Fifth Edition

Mathematics Skill Builder

Loyce C. Gossage, Ed.D.

**Chairman, Accounting and Finance Department
Mt. San Antonio College
Walnut, California**

Published by

M95 SOUTH-WESTERN PUBLISHING CO.

CINCINNATI   WEST CHICAGO, IL   DALLAS   PELHAM MANOR, NY   PALO ALTO, CA

Copyright © 1985

by

SOUTH-WESTERN PUBLISHING CO.

Cincinnati, Ohio

All Rights Reserved

The text of this publication, or any part thereof, may not be reproduced or transmitted in any form or by any means, electronic or mechanical, including photocopying, recording, storage in an information retrieval system, or otherwise, without the prior written permission of the publisher.

Library of Congress

Catalog Card Number: 84-50086

ISBN: 0-538-13950-1

2 3 4 5 6 7 8 K 2 1 0 9 8 7 6

Printed in the United States of America

To the Instructor

Why should a textbook in basic mathematics be revised every few years? Because mathematics, even basic mathematics, is not stagnate; it is continually changing and expanding. Admittedly, basic mathematics does not expand as rapidly as higher mathematics, but it must change because wages, prices, taxes, interest rates, etc., do change, and different concepts move to the forefront.

In addition to containing the usual changes to keep the text realistically compatible with current and future economic problems pertaining to wages, prices, and the like, this Fifth Edition of the MATHEMATICS SKILL BUILDER contains many new lessons designed to introduce simple equations and their use to solve word problems. Also new in this edition are a pretest and a posttest. However, even though this edition contains many new lessons, the primary objectives of this book have not changed. Therefore, those lessons that have been proved in preceding editions to be essential in meeting those objectives are retained in this edition.

This book is planned to help your students achieve the following four objectives:

1. Develop the ability to perform the fundamental operations in mathematics with a high degree of accuracy.
2. Produce results with reasonable speed through the use of practical shortcuts.
3. Establish, by imitation of model script and repetition, the habit of forming clear numerals that are uniform in size.
4. Measure individual progress by use of a unique method of improvement scoring and charting of results in testing.

This book is designed to serve teachers who appreciate the value of a review in the fundamentals of mathematics. It can also be used profitably as a major text in a brief course or as a supplement to any mathematics textbook used in a longer course. This book is recommended for courses in clerical practice, distributive education, general business, and record keeping, as well as for elementary mathematics. It is suitable for young people who are preparing for service in the armed forces, for those who are in practical arts courses, for those preparing for a business occupation or for the business of everyday living, and for those planning to take State or Federal Civil Service entrance examinations.

With this book your students can attain accuracy and build speed in the fundamental operations of addition, subtraction, multiplication, and division. Model script is featured in order to emphasize the importance of neatness and of clear, uniform figures. The correct placement of digits and decimal points is stressed by example.

Measure Improvement. The method of measuring student progress in this book is a distinctive feature. The exercises and tests used in the previous editions and in this edition were tried out with hundreds of students. They were tested to determine the number of problems that could be completed in a given length of time by an average student. The scores were then assigned so that the total possible score attainable on an exercise or test was approximately 200. The time was assigned so that the **average** student, without any preparation, could complete **one half** of an exercise or test and earn a score of 100, which is the **basic score**. The basic score of 100 is then subtracted from the total score. The difference is the **improvement score** because it indicates the improvement that the student has made through study and practice. As a student continues through the book, the improvement scores should rise. In order that the improvement scores may be compared, progress charts are provided on the inside of the front and back covers for the purpose of graphically recording these scores.

Build Enthusiasm. With this book and your guidance, any student who has the will can build mathematical skill. Start your class with a daily drill or test from this book and you will create a "get-down-to-business" attitude at the beginning of every class period. Let the students measure their own progress by means of the improvement scores. Then watch the interest of all your students skyrocket as they experience the joy of progress and achievement!

Acknowledgments. Many of the new lessons and several of the other changes in this edition are the result of suggestions made by many teachers who have used previous editions of this book in their classes. Their constructive assistance is hereby gratefully acknowledged.

Loyce C. Gossage

To the Student

When you have the will, you can develop your skill. With the exercises in this book, you can build a firm foundation in the fundamentals of mathematics so necessary for success in the business world and in the business of everyday living. Just as physical exercise is necessary to build a strong body, so mental exercise is necessary to build an alert mind. This book provides the opportunity for you to develop your ability to use figures accurately and to produce results with reasonable speed.

How to Use This Book. Each exercise in this book is followed by a timed test. Read the explanation and instructions at the top of each page. Practice each exercise until you can complete the exercise in the basic time shown. Then you should be ready to make a satisfactory record in the test given on the back of the sheet. The test is to be worked out only in the presence of your teacher. **No credit will be given for the test if the page is used prior to the period in which your teacher assigns it.**

Many errors in mathematics are due to careless writing of numerals, misplacement of digits and decimal points, and failure to form the habit of checking answers. You can avoid these pitfalls in mathematics if you imitate the model script in your MATHEMATICS SKILL BUILDER, study the shortcuts, and follow the instructions of your teacher for checking your work.

Improvement Scores. In the tests you will not be graded on your total scores, but on your **improvement scores**. For each test, sufficient time is allowed for the average student to obtain a score of 100 — the **basic score** — without previous study. The amount you earn **above** 100 is your **improvement score**. In the upper right-hand corner on each test, there is space for you to record your total score, and to enter the difference between the total score and the basic score which is your improvement score.

For scoring the tests, the value of each correct answer is shown after the instructions when each problem has the same weight. When values are printed at the right of the page, each answer in the row by the value has the same weight. When the value is printed at the bottom of a column and is followed by the word "each," each answer in that column has the value shown. If each answer has a different value, the value is given as near as possible to the space allowed for the answer. Ask your teacher to explain the scoring of any test if you have any question. **Do not remove the test sheet from the book until your teacher instructs you to do so.**

Progress Charts. On the inside front and back covers of this book, you have progress charts on which to keep an accurate record of your improvement scores. Use these charts for the improvement scores on the tests only, not on the practice exercises. The figures at the top and bottom of the charts are the test numbers; the figures at the sides of the charts indicate your possible improvement score for each test. To record your score, use a pen or a colored pencil and fill in the vertical bar for each numbered test until you reach the level that shows the score you have earned. Tall, vertical bars indicate satisfactory progress. Short bars show that you need to spend more time on the practice exercises.

With preparation, practice, and perseverance you can build mathematical skill. Try!

Contents

PRETEST   1

Each exercise is followed by a test that covers the new principles and practical application of the principles presented in the exercise.

Section 1 — Whole Numbers

ADDITION

Exercise

1	Reading and Writing Whole Numbers	3
2	Addition Facts	5
3	Addition of Numbers with More Than One Digit	7
4	Addition of Two-Digit Combinations	9
5	Combinations That Add to 10	11

Exercise

6	Addition of Larger Numbers	13
7	Angular Addition and Subtotaling	15
8	Horizontal Addition	17
9	Vertical and Horizontal Addition	19

SUBTRACTION

10	Subtraction Facts	21
11	Proving Subtraction	23
12	Installment Buying Compared with Cash Buying	25
13	Bank Deposits and Checks	27
14	Customers' Accounts (Accounts Receivable)	29
15	Application Problems	31

MULTIPLICATION

16	Multiplication, 196 Key Combinations	33
17	Multiplication with One-Digit Multipliers	35
18	Multiplication with Two- and Three-Digit Multipliers	37
19	Multiplication with 0 in Multiplicand and in Multiplier	39
20	Checking Multiplication by Casting Out 9's	41
21	Multiplication by 10 and by Multiples of 10	43
22	Application Problems	45

DIVISION

23	Division Facts	47
24	Division with Small Divisors	49
25	Long Division	51
26	Zeros in the Quotient	53
27	Finding Averages	55
28	Application Problems	57

Section 2 — Equations

29	Signed Numbers — Addition and Multiplication	59
30	Signed Numbers — Division and Subtraction	61
31	Solving Equations	63
32	Multiplying and Collecting Terms in Equations	65
33	Order of Operations	67
34	Parentheses in Equations	69
35	Algebraic Expressions	71
36	Application Problems	73

Section 3 — Fractions

DENOMINATORS

37	Common Denominator	75
38	Lowest Terms of Common Fractions	77
39	Improper Fractions and Mixed Numbers	79
40	Lowest Common Denominator	81

ADDITION AND SUBTRACTION

41	Addition of Common Fractions	83
42	Addition of Mixed Numbers	85
43	Subtraction of Common Fractions	87
44	Subtraction of Mixed Numbers	89

Section 3 — Fractions (concluded)

MULTIPLICATION AND DIVISION

Exercise

45	Multiplication of Common Fraction	91
46	Multiplication of Mixed Numbers	93
47	Multiplication of Whole Numbers by Common Fractions	95
48	Division of Common Fractions	97

Exercise

49	Division of Mixed Numbers	99
50	Simplification of Complex Fractions	101
51	Review of Fractions	103
52	Application Problems	105

Section 4 — Decimal Fractions and Aliquot Parts

53	Rounding Numbers	107
54	Equivalent Decimal and Common Fractions	109
55	Decimal Equivalents	111
56	Placement of the Decimal Point	113
57	Figuring a Payroll	115
58	Piecework Payroll	117

59	Division of Decimals	119
60	Shortcut Division by 10 and by Multiples of 10	121
61	Aliquot Parts	123
62	Application Problems	125

Section 5 — Percentage and Selected Business Topics

PERCENTS

63	Percent Equivalents	127
64	Percentage Problems	129

COMMISSIONS

65	Commission on Sales	131
66	Commission on Purchases	133

DISCOUNTS

67	Trade Discounts	135
68	Determining Due Dates	137
69	Cash Discounts	139
70	Discounts on Invoices	141

INTEREST

71	Simple Interest Formula	143
72	Compound Interest	145
73	Application Problems	147

Section 6 — Measurement

UNITED STATES MEASUREMENT

74	U. S. Measurements	149
75	Denominate Numbers	151

METRIC MEASUREMENT

76	Vocabulary of Metric System of Measurement	153
77	Metric Measurements	155
78	Metric Denominates	157
79	Converting from U. S. Measurements to Metric Measurements	159
80	Converting from Metric Measurements to U. S. Measurements	161

POSTTEST 163

TABLE I— U. S. Units of Measure and Their Approximate Metric Equivalents 165

TABLE II— Metric Units of Measure and Their Approximate U. S. Equivalents 167

PRETEST

Name _____ Total Score _____

Date _____ Hour _____

Solve these problems. Place each answer in the appropriate space on the right. Show common fractions in lowest terms. (Score 2 points for each correct answer to Problems 1 through 20 and 3 points for each correct answer to Problems 21 through 40.)

Add:

1. 360
   728
   159
   414
   265

2. $1.50 + 7.82 + 0.08 + 8.96 =$

3. $\dfrac{7}{16}$
   $\dfrac{5}{8}$

4. $19\dfrac{3}{4}$
   $8\dfrac{9}{16}$

Subtract:

5. 7,500
   2,897

6. $9.25 - 3.567 =$

7. $\dfrac{13}{15} - \dfrac{1}{3} =$

8. $8\dfrac{3}{10}$
   $5\dfrac{2}{5}$

Multiply:

9. 865
   407

10. $\dfrac{5}{8} \times 52 =$

11. $\dfrac{7}{13} \times \dfrac{5}{9} =$

12. $18\dfrac{2}{5}$
    $5\dfrac{2}{3}$

13. $70 \times 0.70 =$

14. $2.4 \times 0.8 =$

Divide:

15. $832 \div 8 =$

16. $0.904 \div 0.008 =$

17. $15 \div \dfrac{3}{5} =$

18. $\dfrac{5}{8} \div \dfrac{3}{4} =$

19. $7\dfrac{1}{8} \div 19 =$

20. $4\dfrac{1}{4} \div 8\dfrac{1}{2} =$

1. _____
2. _____
3. _____
4. _____
5. _____
6. _____
7. _____
8. _____
9. _____
10. _____
11. _____
12. _____
13. _____
14. _____
15. _____
16. _____
17. _____
18. _____
19. _____
20. _____

(continued)

PRETEST (concluded)

Write each of the following as a percent:

21. 0.0625
22. $\frac{1}{4}$
23. 4

Write each of the following as a common fraction:

24. 20%
25. $33\frac{1}{3}$%
26. $\frac{1}{2}$%

Write each of the following as a decimal fraction:

27. $1\frac{7}{8}$
28. $12\frac{1}{2}$%

29. Find the average of these daily attendance numbers:

    1,849   1,785   1,862   1,906   1,873

30. Solve this equation: $5(x + 2) - 2(x - 4) = 120$

Solve each of the following:

31. $37\frac{1}{2}$% of 240 = ____?____
32. 30 = 5% of ____?____
33. 18 = ____?____ % of 24
34. Add: 7 hr. 48 min.
         3 hr. 35 min.
35. 23 km = ____?____ m

36. An agent sold a client's shipment of fruit and collected $1,284. The charges were $97.50 for freight and 6% commission for selling. How much should the agent send to the client?..

37. A dealer listed terms of 2/10, n/30 on an invoice for $1,500 worth of goods. How much should the customer pay on April 27 for goods purchased on April 18?..

38. Find the net price for merchandise listed on an invoice at $600 less trade discounts of 20% and 10%..

39. How much is the simple interest on $800 at 14% for eight months?..................

40. A student deposited $900 in an account that pays 16% interest compounded quarterly. Find the compound amount at the end of nine months..................

21. _____
22. _____
23. _____
24. _____
25. _____
26. _____
27. _____
28. _____
29. _____
30. _____
31. _____
32. _____
33. _____
34. _____
35. _____
36. _____
37. _____
38. _____
39. _____
40. _____

Exercise 1: Reading and Writing Whole Numbers

In order to read or write a whole number, arrange its digits in groups (periods) of three digits each. Starting with the first whole digit on the right, insert a comma to the left of each three-digit period. Each period of a number has been named. The group of digits in a period is read as if the period itself were a three-digit number.

The numbers in the chart are read as follows:

	Trillion (Hundreds Tens Ones)	Billion (Hundreds Tens Ones)	Million (Hundreds Tens Ones)	Thousand (Hundreds Tens Ones)	Units (Hundreds Tens Ones)
A					5 6 1
B				7 4 6	5 1 7
C			8	3 1 2	0 4 8
D		4 8	2 5 2	6 3 1	2 3 5
E	8 3 2	0 7 4	0 0 5	0 0 0	0 0 9

A. Five hundred sixty-one. Note on the chart that 5 is in the "hundreds" column, 6 is in the "tens" column, and 1 is in the "ones" column.
B. Seven hundred forty-six **thousand**, five hundred seventeen.
C. Eight **million**, three hundred twelve **thousand**, forty-eight.
D. Forty-eight **billion**, two hundred fifty-two **million**, six hundred thirty-one **thousand**, two hundred thirty-five.
E. Eight hundred thirty-two **trillion**, seventy-four **billion**, five **million**, nine. In reading E, notice that the period representing thousands is not mentioned because the zeros in this period indicate "no thousands."

BASIC TIME — 3½ Minutes

The basic time for each exercise in this book is the estimated time to earn a basic score of 100. It should be possible to complete any exercise in this book in approximately twice the basic time.

Write the following numbers in neat, legible numerals with commas inserted where applicable: (10 each)

1. Seventeen *17*
2. Fifty-four *54*
3. Six hundred seventy-five *675*
4. Seven hundred eighty *780*
5. Four thousand, two hundred seventy-five *4275*
6. Thirteen thousand, two hundred eighty-seven *30287*
7. Nine hundred sixty-two thousand, two hundred six *962206*
8. Three million, four hundred forty thousand, one hundred ninety-one *3*
9. One billion, four million, three thousand, five ....
10. Eight trillion, six billion, four million, two hundred ....
11. Seventy-eight million, sixty-four thousand, nine hundred forty-five ....
12. Seven thousand, fifty *7050*
13. Forty-two thousand, seven *42007*
14. Eighty-nine billion, five hundred thousand, nine hundred eighty ....
15. Six hundred fifty-nine thousand, three hundred twenty-four *659324*
16. Four hundred fifty-three billion, nine hundred three million, six hundred ninety-two thousand, ninety ....
17. Seventy-five trillion, sixty-two million, twelve thousand ....
18. Eight hundred eighty million, nine hundred five thousand, six hundred eleven ....
19. Sixty-three billion, five hundred eighty million, fifty-eight thousand, ninety-six ....
20. Three hundred seventy-six million, nine hundred seventy-one thousand, seven hundred forty ....

Test 1

Name _____
Date _____
Basic Time — 3 Minutes

Total Score _____
Basic Score ___100___
Improvement Score _____

You should be able to score 100 on this test in 3 minutes. The amount you earn above 100 is your **improvement score**. The improvement scores for Tests 1 through 40 should be recorded on the Progress Chart on the inside of the front cover, and the improvement scores for Tests 41 through 80 should be recorded on the inside of the back cover. Record this test as the first vertical bar on the inside front cover for Test 1.

Write these numbers in neat, legible numerals and insert commas where applicable: (10 each)

1. Fourteen .... _____
2. Eighty-seven .... _____
3. Eight hundred twenty-seven .... _____
4. One hundred thirty-one .... _____
5. Eleven thousand, three hundred fourteen .... _____
6. Seventy-five thousand, eighty .... _____
7. Two hundred nine thousand, five .... _____
8. Four million, fifty-five thousand, two hundred forty-eight .... _____
9. Sixty-six million, seven hundred ninety-nine thousand, two hundred twenty-seven .... _____
10. Four hundred one million, eight thousand, sixty .... _____
11. Seventy billion, one hundred seventy-three million, two hundred one thousand, one hundred .... _____
12. Eighty-four billion, five hundred two million, four hundred eight thousand, five hundred nine .... _____
13. Five hundred sixty-one billion, eight hundred eight million, sixty-five thousand, four .... _____
14. Nineteen trillion, five hundred billion, eight hundred million, seven thousand .... _____
15. Thirty trillion, seven hundred sixty-two million, five hundred eighteen .... _____
16. Forty thousand, five hundred .... _____
17. Two billion, one hundred fifty-nine thousand, three hundred fifty-eight .... _____
18. Two hundred billion, five hundred sixty-eight million, thirty .... _____
19. Seventy-nine billion, two hundred fifty million, two hundred fifty-six thousand, one hundred forty-eight .... _____
20. Eight million five .... _____

Exercise 2 — Addition Facts

Addition is combining two or more numbers (the **addends**) to obtain an answer (the **sum** or **total**).

The secret of speed and accuracy in addition is recognizing combinations of numbers as totals, just as combinations of letters are recognized as words. Using 0, 1, 2, 3, 4, 5, 6, 7, 8, and 9, there are 100 combinations of two numbers. These combinations are shown below. Study them thoroughly, left to right, up and down, and on the diagonal, to learn all the combinations of these numbers. Although this exercise is a very simple one, it will form part of your mathematical background for future work.

The diagonal rows show the combinations that form the totals from 1 to 10. The combinations on the diagonal row for 10 are very important to learn, because they will be in another exercise.

Practice this exercise until you can complete it in less than one minute.

BASIC TIME — $\frac{3}{4}$ Minute (Estimated time to obtain a basic score of 100)

Add: (2 each)

	a	b	c	d	e	f	g	h	i	j	
	0	1	2	3	4	5	6	7	8	9	
1.	0/0	1/0	2/0	3/0	4/0	5/0	6/0	7/0	8/0	9/0	10
2.	0/1	1/1	2/1	3/1	4/1	5/1	6/1	7/1	8/1	9/1	11
3.	0/2	1/2	2/2	3/2	4/2	5/2	6/2	7/2	8/2	9/2	12
4.	0/3	1/3	2/3	3/3	4/3	5/3	6/3	7/3	8/3	9/3	13
5.	0/4	1/4	2/4	3/4	4/4	5/4	6/4	7/4	8/4	9/4	14
6.	0/5	1/5	2/5	3/5	4/5	5/5	6/5	7/5	8/5	9/5	15
7.	0/6	1/6	2/6	3/6	4/6	5/6	6/6	7/6	8/6	9/6	16
8.	0/7	1/7	2/7	3/7	4/7	5/7	6/7	7/7	8/7	9/7	17
9.	0/8	1/8	2/8	3/8	4/8	5/8	6/8	7/8	8/8	9/8	18
10.	0/9	1/9	2/9	3/9	4/9	5/9	6/9	7/9	8/9	9/9	

Test 2

Name _____
Date _____
Basic Time — ¾ Minute

Total Score _____
Basic Score   100
Improvement Score _____

Add: (2 each)

	a	b	c	d	e	f	g	h	i	j
1.	9 8	8 6	5 9	6 3	3 8	8 4	8 3	9 5	4 5	9 2
2.	3 2	5 8	3 3	4 8	9 9	2 1	8 0	4 7	0 9	7 1
3.	1 0	8 8	6 6	2 4	3 6	2 5	3 0	2 3	8 5	5 3
4.	9 6	4 0	1 6	7 7	5 4	2 0	0 8	1 1	9 4	5 0
5.	0 7	7 0	7 8	6 7	4 1	1 5	2 8	8 9	9 7	3 5
6.	8 7	0 3	3 9	2 2	9 1	7 9	9 3	0 2	2 7	1 3
7.	3 1	6 5	7 4	2 6	6 0	1 9	6 9	5 6	6 2	8 2
8.	6 8	5 1	1 7	7 6	3 4	6 4	9 0	7 2	8 1	4 9
9.	4 2	7 5	4 3	7 3	1 8	4 6	5 7	5 5	0 6	6 1
10.	5 2	1 4	0 5	4 4	1 2	0 4	3 7	2 9	0 1	0 0

Exercise 3: Addition of Numbers with More Than One Digit

The Arabic numerals 1–9 (and sometimes 0) are referred to as **digits**. This drill combines the addition of one-digit and two-digit numbers. When the digits in the right column total more than 9, a digit must be carried over to the next column on the left. It is helpful to write this digit over the left column so it will not be forgotten.

The example shows the carrying of the digit 1. When adding 16 and 8, the digit 1 is carried over to the "tens" column from the total of 14 in the "ones" column. Before actually writing the answers, add these numbers mentally for practice in addition.

```
 1
16
 8
――
24
```

BASIC TIME — 1 Minute *(Estimated time to obtain a basic score of 100)*

Add: (2 each)

	a	b	c	d	e	f	g	h	i	j
1.	11	15	18	12	17	14	19	16	13	18
	2	9	7	5	8	6	4	1	5	9
2.	23	2	21	1	28	7	29	6	26	9
	4	26	3	25	8	24	5	22	8	27
3.	1	8	7	6	4	2	9	5	3	7
	37	34	32	39	31	35	38	33	36	38
4.	41	1	42	2	44	7	46	6	48	9
	5	48	8	47	9	49	4	43	5	46
5.	5	52	1	59	7	4	58	51	9	53
	56	9	54	8	53	55	2	6	58	9
6.	62	66	7	4	69	64	3	5	64	68
	1	6	61	67	9	2	68	65	6	6
7.	6	72	76	9	4	77	88	8	9	6
	75	2	7	73	78	5	5	86	84	75
8.	87	7	4	9	99	93	97	6	5	7
	6	85	92	96	3	2	7	98	98	96
9.	3	27	36	45	3	8	2	95	38	7
	13	9	3	3	57	63	89	8	3	26
10.	23	9	42	7	69	8	97	9	9	97
	6	34	7	59	4	77	5	95	88	9

7

Test 3

Name _____ Total Score _____

Date _____ Basic Score _____100_____

Basic Time — 1 Minute   Improvement Score _____

Add: (2 each)

	a	b	c	d	e	f	g	h	i	j
1.	11	26	32	47	53	64	79	85	96	37
	9	7	5	8	6	4	3	1	2	5
2.	4	2	3	1	8	7	5	6	9	8
	15	21	39	44	55	68	71	81	89	46
3.	25	8	49	6	63	2	12	5	39	7
	1	31	7	58	4	77	9	28	6	38
4.	5	51	2	17	9	38	4	57	9	47
	46	1	65	8	24	7	43	6	75	6
5.	29	33	1	8	22	36	2	6	64	5
	5	9	45	19	7	4	16	27	8	37
6.	1	6	42	59	9	2	87	98	3	5
	23	34	7	4	69	74	3	8	98	59
7.	48	54	7	78	83	3	41	52	4	28
	6	2	67	9	4	91	1	8	37	6
8.	4	5	97	3	2	76	6	7	49	8
	73	89	8	56	66	1	82	94	5	39
9.	72	86	93	2	5	7	84	96	57	3
	4	9	3	75	88	99	1	6	9	37
10.	2	18	3	14	5	61	3	62	5	9
	95	9	35	3	37	5	13	9	36	47

Exercise 4: Addition of Two-Digit Combinations

If you have thoroughly mastered the simple combinations, you will not find it difficult to add combinations of two numbers with two digits each.

Since the digits in the "ones" column of each number cannot be larger than 9 plus 9, with a total of 18, the digit 1 is the largest digit to be carried. This is carried over in the same way as explained in Exercise 3.

Go through the work one or more times mentally before writing the answers.

BASIC TIME — 2 Minutes *(Estimated time to obtain a basic score of 100)*

Add: (2 each)

	a	b	c	d	e	f	g	h	i	j
1.	38 21	57 32	45 34	32 25	42 54	31 28	65 27	83 15	64 28	39 29
2.	28 49	83 46	37 86	29 45	34 28	93 15	47 68	25 39	23 88	74 23
3.	68 49	56 71	64 28	39 42	37 61	59 83	74 16	19 47	65 87	98 43
4.	37 22	59 76	83 24	55 99	24 13	82 71	55 29	82 36	56 49	39 26
5.	93 14	26 53	29 84	53 28	28 73	47 26	84 29	31 45	75 78	93 28
6.	78 25	37 69	82 14	73 69	84 28	62 48	92 15	73 16	29 33	34 69
7.	59 67	32 49	55 63	87 91	48 26	53 97	45 57	63 98	37 69	84 57
8.	23 89	74 25	93 25	68 54	83 17	75 29	36 83	24 47	71 98	64 36
9.	61 28	24 57	28 16	74 28	68 93	95 82	49 87	63 29	62 79	65 97
10.	54 78	69 23	51 28	46 83	72 96	47 84	26 75	38 44	83 29	58 46

Test 4

10

Name		Total Score	
Date		Basic Score	100
Basic Time — 2 Minutes		Improvement Score	

Add: (2 each)

	a	b	c	d	e	f	g	h	i	j
1.	39 83	57 37	45 29	63 34	42 93	31 47	65 25	83 24	83 64	57 69
2.	28 56	21 46	32 86	34 45	25 28	54 15	28 68	27 39	96 69	28 37
3.	28 49	49 71	64 55	39 24	37 82	59 55	74 82	19 74	72 59	82 77
4.	37 26	59 29	83 53	28 99	42 13	61 71	83 29	16 36	85 63	57 64
5.	22 53	76 84	24 28	28 62	47 92	84 73	31 95	68 39	84 73	95 68
6.	37 55	82 87	73 48	84 53	75 49	26 15	29 16	45 82	25 88	47 29
7.	82 67	61 68	15 57	28 93	47 28	78 32	93 67	27 42	62 98	25 89
8.	43 56	94 26	87 49	25 36	83 29	75 68	26 84	92 97	87 49	38 57
9.	82 84	78 68	23 77	49 59	68 73	28 29	17 26	53 74	84 59	68 46
10.	73 28	26 81	19 27	34 26	82 15	73 68	92 51	73 26	79 82	87 29

Exercise 5: Combinations That Add to 10

Up to now, the problems have been limited to the addition of two numbers. When adding more than two numbers, there are instances when two digits that add to 10 come together. Form the habit of recognizing these combinations as 10 and adding them in a single operation. Grouping combinations that add to 10 will greatly increase both your accuracy and speed.

In this exercise, each problem contains at least one combination of 10. Be extremely careful to avoid overlooking the numerals that are not included in the combination. At first, indicating these combinations as illustrated will be helpful.

In the first four drills below, combinations of 10 are connected by lines. In the fifth drill, you are to connect the combinations by lines before adding.

BASIC TIME — 2½ Minutes *(Estimated time to obtain a basic score of 100)*

Add:

	a	b	c	d	e	f	g	h	i	j	k	l
1.	6	8	7	8	9	5	5	3	1	6	8	5
	4	9	4	2	3	5	3	6	6	8	7	9
	7	1	6	7	7	8	5	7	9	4	2	5

(2)

	a	b	c	d	e	f	g	h	i	j	k	l
2.	3	6	1	4	3	2	3	2	3	7	9	3
	7	4	8	6	9	8	6	9	6	6	5	6
	2	2	9	2	6	4	7	7	4	3	2	7
	1	8	1	7	4	6	2	1	8	8	5	4
	4	4	5	8	3	7	8	4	3	6	8	2
	6	4	5	2	7	9	3	6	2	2	4	6

(4)

	a	b	c	d	e	f	g	h
3.	33	32	77	39	44	28	36	67
	67	26	32	81	57	41	81	38
	42	84	28	76	63	82	74	43

(4)

	a	b	c	d	e	f	g	h
4.	82	47	74	18	75	83	32	99
	78	63	36	92	48	26	79	81
	32	82	46	47	35	77	21	47
	18	28	87	63	62	47	64	23
	96	99	23	93	51	32	86	64
	54	51	45	27	48	63	23	86

(8)

Connect the combinations of 10 by lines and add:

	a	b	c	d	e	f	g	h
5.	64	72	72	87	26	38	41	24
	78	39	38	29	17	29	59	56
	32	32	25	41	84	72	67	87

(4)

Test 5

Name		Total Score	
Date		Basic Score	100
Basic Time — 2½ Minutes		Improvement Score	

Add:

	a	b	c	d	e	f	g	h	i	j	k	l
1.	6 4 8	7 2 8	9 3 7	9 1 8	5 5 6	5 6 4	1 8 9	6 2 4	5 9 5	3 9 7	8 9 2	2 7 8

(2)

	a	b	c	d	e	f	g	h	i	j	k	l
2.	3 7 2 8 2 5	7 4 6 7 8 2	9 1 8 2 4 8	7 1 9 2 8 4	6 9 8 2 4 6	8 2 4 6 3 8	9 1 4 7 6 3	7 4 4 6 6 2	1 6 4 9 8 1	2 6 4 8 9 2	3 7 4 6 8 4	7 8 3 5 7 5

(4)

	a	b	c	d	e	f	g	h
3.	54 56 24	38 71 49	84 29 31	73 28 82	92 47 18	27 49 83	73 56 34	29 84 11

(4)

	a	b	c	d	e	f	g	h
4.	16 74 33 29 81 52	36 44 68 82 26 34	83 27 49 62 88 23	37 63 47 29 81 67	64 26 82 51 59 35	36 27 74 23 85 35	78 29 32 81 56 64	78 22 31 75 66 45

(8)

Connect the combinations of 10 by lines and add:

	a	b	c	d	e	f	g	h
5.	36 49 61	83 37 72	65 45 82	74 56 52	29 41 87	65 25 43	72 47 68	39 81 74

(4)

Exercise 6: Addition of Larger Numbers

The addition of numbers with three digits or more is presented here to develop greater speed and accuracy. Form the habit of making legible numbers and keeping digits in a straight column. Insert commas where necessary.

In adding digits that total over 9, be sure to carry a digit over to the next column on the left.

In the example at the right, the digit 1 is carried over from the far right column to the middle column. The digit 1 is again carried over from the middle column to the left column.

It helps to write at the top of the column the digit which is carried to that column.

```
 11
234
587
---
821
```

BASIC TIME — 2 Minutes *(Estimated time to obtain a basic score of 100)*

Add:

	a	b	c	d	e	f
1.	345 698	254 736	829 847	378 692	574 692	925 381 (4)
2.	748 642	293 718	786 692	267 541	493 386	254 255 (4)
3.	843 927	298 354	674 732	235 872	368 645	758 452 (4)

	a	b	c	d
4.	642,865 921,565	784,228 843,627	372,486 687,769	478,695 341,217 (8)

	a	b	c
5.	742,618,726 427,864,415	427,893,876 738,264,699	924,647,822 376,256,878 (12)
6.	423,876,982 839,213,469	476,827,698 928,022,809	247,692,385 786,427,820 (12)
7.	294,391 748,692	249,382 389,827	831,476 978,937 (8)

Test 6

Name _____ Total Score _____
Date _____ Basic Score   100
Basic Time — 2 Minutes Improvement Score _____

Add:

	a	b	c	d	e	f	
1.	786 394	928 782	475 698	378 257	689 836	546 921	(4)
2.	378 269	543 786	834 729	541 269	786 293	548 687	(4)
3.	287 465	387 298	546 589	728 569	834 785	692 847	(4)

	a	b	c	d	
4.	683,945 821,596	382,769 737,892	473,586 469,218	592,768 409,826	(8)

	a	b	c	
5.	725,678,296 854,927,707	537,698,276 654,276,987	547,692,859 382,769,842	(12)
6.	138,925,467 426,178,698	293,847,693 542,769,827	786,925,478 354,769,842	(12)
7.	392,844 547,276	693,295 248,708	476,698 781,786	(8)

Exercise 7 — Angular Addition and Subtotaling

Electronic calculators are commonly used today for the addition of long columns. You should not, however, be completely dependent on electronic methods in mathematics. Two methods that are used to simplify addition and to check accuracy are: (1) angular addition and (2) subtotaling.

In angular addition, add each column of numerals separately. Then add the totals together (Example A). A somewhat difficult problem can be thought of as being three easier problems.

In subtotaling, obtain subtotals for parts of a long problem and add the subtotals (Example B).

Example A

```
274   2  7  4   274
685   6  8  5   685
396   3  9  6   396
721   7  2  1   721
805   8  0  5   805
540   5  4  0   540
3,421 31 30 21   21
                 30
                 31
              3,421
```

Example B

```
663   663
329   329
816   816
576   576
588   588  2,972 subtotal
228   228
867   867
872   872
854   854
647   647  3,468 subtotal
6,440      6,440 total
```

BASIC TIME — 12 Minutes *(Estimated time to obtain a basic score of 100)*

1. Add the following problems by adding each column of numerals separately. Then add the columnar totals to obtain the total:

	a	b	c	d	e
	272	944	357	8,123	2,774
	107	775	106	7,510	7,887
	814	753	197	1,085	3,551
	760	107	371	6,534	4,560
	591	779	810	9,469	5,494
	467	107	849	3,638	1,745
	157	811	693	1,086 (24)	8,361 (24)
	724 (16)	661 (16)	556 (16)		

2. Determine the totals of the following problems by first finding subtotals:

a	b	c	d
344	608	8,275	6,890
362	758	2,618	7,284
362	515	1,034	3,438
482	924	2,682	6,754
337	656	1,056	3,204
628	594	7,514	4,505
324	464	6,791	5,463
248	867	4,151	7,207
842	464	5,706	4,754
183	876	7,125	8,923
968	528	3,506	9,257
876 (24)	252 (24)	8,898 (28)	8,373 (28)

Test 7

16

Name _____ Total Score _____
Date _____ Basic Score   **100**
Basic Time — 10 Minutes   Improvement Score _____

1. Use angular addition to find these sums:

a	b	c	d	e
494	165	618	8,649	7,099
847	559	622	7,856	9,592
511	428	159	4,822	3,683
577	135	285	4,776	9,971
905	650	341	6,252	1,617
699	417	375	2,791	2,193
359	505	662	8,679 (24)	8,062 (24)
424 (16)	876 (16)	996 (16)		

2. Add by first determining subtotals:

a	b	c	d
642	716	4,525	9,372
890	649	5,477	1,047
109	352	1,010	8,154
183	250	4,820	1,979
106	902	3,560	6,029
717 ____	942 ____	3,929	2,276
547	600	2,131 ____	3,411 ____
811	656	2,894	6,776
929	656	5,240	1,014
461	455	7,372	7,798
879	107	9,570	9,512
735	615	5,385	5,699
792 ____	649 ____	3,415	2,318
		1,121 ____	3,421 ____
		3,705	1,547
		4,370	4,135
		4,216	2,035
		4,216	4,035
		9,696	4,265
		1,383	9,616
		8,956 ____	8,999 ____

(20)　　　(20)　　　(32)　　　(32)

Exercise 8 — Horizontal Addition

Numbers to be added do not always appear in vertical columns. They are sometimes arranged horizontally. Such an arrangement reduces speed in addition. You need practice, therefore, in horizontal addition. Be on the alert to group combinations of 10 when adding the digits in horizontal columns. This will increase both your speed and accuracy.

When numbers to be added are included in a paragraph of reading matter, write them in vertical columns before adding them to insure accuracy.

BASIC TIME — 3 Minutes *(Estimated time to obtain a basic score of 100)*

Add: (14 each)

1. 3+4+6+9+5+3+7+4+2+8+5+7+6+4+8 = _____
2. 7+8+9+1+6+8+2+5+7+3+8+2+9+8+7 = _____
3. 8+5+3+7+9+2+8+7+5+4+2+1+3+7+6 = _____
4. 5+2+8+9+3+7+6+5+8+7+6+4+2+5+3 = _____
5. 6+4+2+7+3+2+1+9+3+2+4+7+6+8+5 = _____
6. 2+5+9+6+4+9+3+2+1+3+9+6+8+4+2 = _____
7. 5+2+7+6+9+3+2+5+8+7+9+3+5+8+6 = _____
8. 2+4+6+9+3+2+1+4+7+9+8+4+3+2+5 = _____
9. 5+6+7+1+4+2+8+9+3+7+6+7+8+4+3 = _____
10. 9+8+7+5+4+8+9+7+6+8+9+8+7+8+9 = _____

11. The following number of newspapers were sold from a coin-operated stand: 38 papers on Monday; 39 on Tuesday; 43 on Wednesday; 45 on Thursday; 41 on Friday; and 72 on Saturday. How many newspapers were sold during the week? .... _____ (16)

12. The sales of a store were as follows: Monday, $26,547; Tuesday, $32,765; Wednesday, $27,530; Thursday, $31,080; Friday, $21,565; Saturday, $17,575. Find the total sales for the week .... _____ (44)

Test 8

Name		Total Score	
Date		Basic Score	100
Basic Time — 4 Minutes		Improvement Score	

Find the sum of the digits composing each of the following numbers: (4 each)

	a	b	c	d
1.	347609 = _____	576289 = _____	937684 = _____	571027 = _____
2.	561908 = _____	746841 = _____	625376 = _____	985769 = _____
3.	737689 = _____	397692 = _____	769589 = _____	768675 = _____
4.	624756 = _____	656897 = _____	562145 = _____	695210 = _____
5.	721041 = _____	714685 = _____	312567 = _____	869265 = _____

Compute the total hours worked by each person for each week: (4 each)

RECORD OF HOURS WORKED

	Employee	1st Week M	T	W	Th	F	S	Total Hours	2d Week M	T	W	Th	F	S	Total Hours
6.	Arroyo, Lydia	8	9	8	8	9	5		8	8	9	7	8	5	
7.	Behler, Gregg	8	8	8	7	8	5		8	9	8	8	8	5	
8.	Deane, Maxine	9	8	9	8	7	5		9	9	8	9	8	5	
9.	Grau, William	8	9	8	8	8	4		9	8	9	8	8	5	
10.	Hunter, Ellen	8	8	8	9	8	5		7	8	8	8	7	5	
11.	Leon, Juan	8	6	4	9	9	5		8	8	9	9	6	5	
12.	Mills, Jason	9	8	9	8	8	5		9	8	9	9	8	5	
13.	Newman, Beth	8	8	7	8	9	5		8	9	7	8	9	5	
14.	Okana, Benji	6	9	8	8	7	4		8	8	8	9	8	4	
15.	Paul, Joseph	9	8	8	9	8	5		9	8	8	8	9	5	
16.	Ranz, Carole	8	7	8	8	8	5		8	8	9	8	9	4	
17.	Siegel, Lois	9	9	8	7	8	5		8	7	8	9	9	5	
18.	Tepe, Janice	8	8	9	8	9	4		9	8	7	8	8	5	
19.	Vehr, Ellen	8	8	9	8	9	5		8	9	8	8	8	6	
20.	Yang, Tom	9	9	8	9	8	6		9	8	9	9	6	4	

Exercise 9: Vertical and Horizontal Addition

Frequently in business, groups of numbers must be added both horizontally and vertically. Records of daily cash receipts and daily expense account summaries are examples of this type of addition.

An excellent means of proving the accuracy of such addition is to verify that the grand total of the sums of the vertical columns equals the total of the sums of the horizontal rows. A single error at any point, of course, makes this equality impossible.

Be very careful when adding horizontally to add together only those digits in the same position in each column of numbers.

BASIC TIME — 15 Minutes *(Estimated time to obtain a basic score of 100)*

Add horizontally and vertically: (14 points for No. 14; 4 points for other correct answers)

1.	375	24	8	326	493	7	62	
2.	47	45	549	9	381	74	874	
3.	682	394	27	7	742	88	68	
4.	3	27	684	548	29	926	29	
5.	927	6	57	9	574	54	385	
6.	63	983	8	28	689	72	7	
	7.	8.	9.	10.	11.	12.	13.	14.

Add horizontally and vertically: (20 points for No. 34; 6 points for other correct answers)

CASH RECEIPTS

	Route Number	Mon.	Tues.	Wed.	Thurs.	Fri.	Weekly Total
15.	1	45 11	50 19	19 72	40 44	70 12	
16.	2	53 10	40 12	32 19	60 12	79 42	
17.	3	39 12	50 26	30 91	87 21	67 63	
18.	4	42 40	24 04	36 40	89 42	96 19	
19.	5	38 67	36 60	43 90	77 09	86 41	
20.	6	29 05	47 29	40 41	87 90	91 11	
21.	7	30 17	37 02	40 04	97 82	97 36	
22.	8	51 42	49 11	48 19	98 64	92 42	
23.	9	19 09	38 05	49 71	89 46	68 50	
24.	10	35 04	60 51	30 65	74 11	72 76	
25.	11	28 29	37 10	49 11	79 32	84 62	
26.	12	32 22	43 32	50 09	84 47	93 99	
27.	13	29 40	32 34	56 14	91 10	92 84	
	14	41 13	23 40	48 39	88 05	85 01	
	Daily Total						
		29.	30.	31.	32.	33.	34.

Test 9

Name		Total Score	
Date		Basic Score	100
Basic Time — 15 Minutes		Improvement Score	

Add horizontally and vertically: (10 points for Nos. 16 and 32; 2 points for other correct answers)

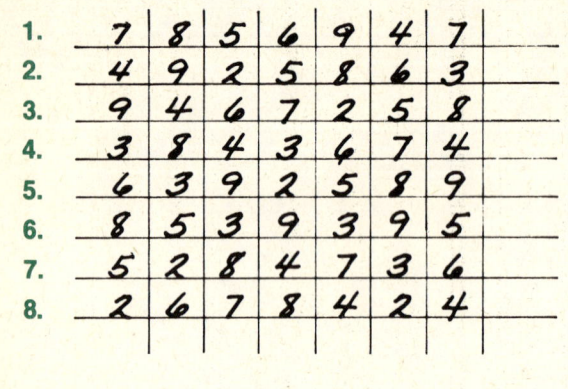

1.	7	8	5	6	9	4	7		17.	5	9	4	3	8	2	8
2.	4	9	2	5	8	6	3		18.	2	8	7	4	6	5	3
3.	9	4	6	7	2	5	8		19.	7	4	9	6	8	2	5
4.	3	8	4	3	6	7	4		20.	6	7	3	2	7	8	9
5.	6	3	9	2	5	8	9		21.	3	2	5	7	5	6	7
6.	8	5	3	9	3	9	5		22.	8	5	8	5	9	7	4
7.	5	2	8	4	7	3	6		23.	4	6	2	8	4	9	6
8.	2	6	7	8	4	2	4		24.	9	8	6	9	7	6	8

9. 10. 11. 12. 13. 14. 15. 16.   25. 26. 27. 28. 29. 30. 31. 32.

Some business organizations offer their salespeople bonuses, usually in the form of extra cash commissions, on all sales exceeding set amounts.

Four salespeople earned bonuses for additional sales as shown below. Find the total bonuses paid by the firm during each month, the total bonus earned by each salesperson during the year, and the grand total of bonuses paid during the year. (24 points for No. 49; 6 points for other correct answers)

	MONTH	BLANCO	CRUZ	DIAZ	MEDINA	TOTAL
33.	January	54 16	78 26	85 42	38 46	
34.	February	38 29	71 74	80 26	35 27	
35.	March	55 22	76 49	86 34	40 22	
36.	April	83 12	86 40	84 26	41 24	
37.	May	50 82	73 21	79 47	37 69	
38.	June	125 78	137 60	112 30	51 37	
39.	July	39 84	70 24	76 40	35 12	
40.	August	32 26	36 54	72 37	30 26	
41.	September	47 59	69 25	79 26	30 48	
42.	October	57 26	79 40	87 47	39 12	
43.	November	52 47	81 25	88 37	40 46	
44.	December	142 75	168 47	155 22	75 29	
	TOTAL	45.	46.	47.	48.	49.

Exercise 10 — Subtraction Facts

Addition is the first fundamental operation in mathematics. Subtraction, the process of finding the difference between two numbers, is the second fundamental operation. The top number is the **minuend**. The bottom number is the **subtrahend**. The answer is the **difference** or **remainder**.

These terms are illustrated in the example at the right.

This exercise contains 100 basic combinations for subtraction. Study them, left to right, up and down, and on the diagonal, to learn them thoroughly.

```
 14  minuend
  5  subtrahend
 ―――
  9  difference
```

BASIC TIME — 3/4 Minute *(Estimated time to obtain a basic score of 100)*

Subtract: (2 each)

	a	b	c	d	e	f	g	h	i	j
1.	0−0	1−0	2−0	3−0	4−0	5−0	6−0	7−0	8−0	9−0
2.	1−1	2−1	3−1	4−1	5−1	6−1	7−1	8−1	9−1	10−1
3.	2−2	3−2	4−2	5−2	6−2	7−2	8−2	9−2	10−2	11−2
4.	3−3	4−3	5−3	6−3	7−3	8−3	9−3	10−3	11−3	12−3
5.	4−4	5−4	6−4	7−4	8−4	9−4	10−4	11−4	12−4	13−4
6.	5−5	6−5	7−5	8−5	9−5	10−5	11−5	12−5	13−5	14−5
7.	6−6	7−6	8−6	9−6	10−6	11−6	12−6	13−6	14−6	15−6
8.	7−7	8−7	9−7	10−7	11−7	12−7	13−7	14−7	15−7	16−7
9.	8−8	9−8	10−8	11−8	12−8	13−8	14−8	15−8	16−8	17−8
10.	9−9	10−9	11−9	12−9	13−9	14−9	15−9	16−9	17−9	18−9

Test 10

Name _____ Total Score _____
Date _____ Basic Score   100
Basic Time — 3/4 Minute Improvement Score _____

Subtract: (2 each)

	a	b	c	d	e	f	g	h	i	j
1.	9 − 7	10 − 2	13 − 5	0 − 0	12 − 9	9 − 9	11 − 5	12 − 7	5 − 0	16 − 8
2.	6 − 0	9 − 0	10 − 1	13 − 8	11 − 2	14 − 9	8 − 3	6 − 4	16 − 7	13 − 7
3.	15 − 6	11 − 9	9 − 5	4 − 2	14 − 6	8 − 4	8 − 1	7 − 3	12 − 5	9 − 1
4.	14 − 8	8 − 7	4 − 0	5 − 5	7 − 1	5 − 2	12 − 6	2 − 1	4 − 3	8 − 6
5.	11 − 8	7 − 0	9 − 4	3 − 1	13 − 9	10 − 3	11 − 7	6 − 6	14 − 7	17 − 9
6.	9 − 8	11 − 6	16 − 9	5 − 1	7 − 7	12 − 3	7 − 5	17 − 8	10 − 8	13 − 4
7.	9 − 3	8 − 8	10 − 6	3 − 3	8 − 2	6 − 5	5 − 3	1 − 1	12 − 4	8 − 5
8.	4 − 1	6 − 1	7 − 2	8 − 0	10 − 9	10 − 4	18 − 9	7 − 4	4 − 4	6 − 3
9.	12 − 8	9 − 2	2 − 0	6 − 2	3 − 0	11 − 3	1 − 0	10 − 5	15 − 9	3 − 2
10.	11 − 4	2 − 2	14 − 5	15 − 7	10 − 7	5 − 4	13 − 6	15 − 8	7 − 6	9 − 6

Exercise 11 — Proving Subtraction

Checking subtraction through addition is easy. This is done by adding the *difference* to the *subtrahend*. The sum of these two numbers must equal the *minuend* if the answer is correct.

You may need to "borrow" from the "tens" column when subtracting. If 46 is subtracted from 81, as shown in the example at the right, the 6 cannot be subtracted from 1. Therefore a 10 is borrowed from the "tens" column and is added to the 1, making 11. Then 6 is subtracted from 11 to get 5. Four is subtracted from the remaining 7 in the "tens" column to get 3, and the answer is 35. The check of the answer is also shown in the example.

```
  7
 ₈1      35
-46     +46
 ──     ──
 35      81
```

BASIC TIME — 6 Minutes *(Estimated time to obtain a basic score of 100)*

Write the differences and prove answers: (202 points)

	a	b	c	d	e	f	g	h
1.	91 45	121 74	102 57	143 79	203 98	111 67	129 58	120 83	(3)
2.	41 25	71 42	85 73	124 93	84 56	131 82	68 47	111 57	(3)
3.	103 84	86 29	72 37	88 69	92 47	132 85	91 53	55 26	(3)

	a	b	c	d	e
4.	10,342 7,264	8,223 6,789	6,228 5,769	10,422 8,360	8,327 4,679	(6)
5.	11,251 5,698	8,129 7,643	5,762 1,915	10,212 9,487	9,215 3,746	(6)
6.	8,201 2,405	9,473 3,245	7,692 1,038	9,520 4,371	9,000 8,371	(6)

	a	b	c	d
7.	81,245 53,627	746,210 123,798	151,627 92,745	1,007,618 308,247	(10)

Test 11

Name _____
Date _____
Basic Time — 5 Minutes

Total Score _____
Basic Score ___100___
Improvement Score _____

1. Write in the differences and prove the answers:

a	b	c	d	e	f	g	h	i	j
64	93	81	112	102	75	111	73	113	93
29	57	54	78	65	36	89	48	24	56

(5)

2. Stephen is 19 years old. His grandfather is 72 years old. His father is 43 years old.

   (a) How many years younger is Stephen than his grandfather?............................... _____ (10)

   (b) How many years younger than his father? .... _____ (10)

   (c) How many years older is his grandfather than his father?................................ _____ (10)

3. Write in the differences and prove the answers:

a	b	c	d	e	f
5,168	9,038	7,463	6,597	7,189	8,656
3,583	7,149	5,675	2,742	4,672	2,458

(10)

4. A market's June sales amounted to $647,894; July sales, $812,635; August sales, $756,946.

   (a) What were the total sales for the three months?............................ _____ (20)

   (b) July sales were how much more than June sales? .... _____ (20)

   (c) August sales were how much more than June sales?..................... _____ (20)

Exercise 12 — Installment Buying Compared with Cash Buying

People who do not have ready cash often buy furniture and equipment for their homes on the installment plan. This plan provides for payment of the purchase price in small amounts over a period of months. Cash prices are almost always lower than installment prices; thus, you and your family can save money by purchasing with cash.

In this exercise, horizontal subtraction must be used to find the difference between the installment price and the cash price — the amount that is saved through a cash purchase. Record the saving (the difference) in the right-hand column. Be careful to subtract only those digits that are in the same position in each column of numbers.

BASIC TIME — 4 Minutes *(Estimated time to obtain a basic score of 100)*

Subtract horizontally: (10 each)

	ITEM	INSTALLMENT PRICE	CASH PRICE	SAVING
1.	Refrigerator	799 99	698 98	
2.	Television set	987 50	899 25	
3.	Vacuum cleaner	215 40	179 50	
4.	Washer	629 90	589 99	
5.	Microwave cart	89 00	74 95	
6.	Electric dryer	589 00	459 45	
7.	Student's desk	195 75	169 95	
8.	Living room chair	339 55	277 77	
9.	Sewing machine	393 72	325 39	
10.	Cassette player	239 95	199 50	
11.	Dinette	805 19	659 99	
12.	Rocking chair	160 89	138 70	
13.	Twin bed	175 00	149 98	
14.	Bedroom dresser	268 95	236 40	
15.	Electric cooktop unit	295 00	279 50	
16.	Living room sofa	569 95	448 45	
17.	Metal bookcase	229 00	189 00	
18.	Bunk bed	324 88	282 50	
19.	Microwave oven	720 12	686 55	
20.	Video recorder	985 00	869 95	

Test 12

Name _____ Total Score _____
Date _____ Basic Score ____100____
Basic Time — 4 Minutes Improvement Score _____

Record the saving: (10 each)

	ITEM	INSTALLMENT PRICE	CASH PRICE	SAVING
1.	Area rug	198 50	179 95	
2.	Dinnerware set	299 00	275 50	
3.	Food processor	85 00	79 95	
4.	Electric range	710 66	577 77	
5.	Air conditioner	953 98	799 99	
6.	Swivel chair	189 80	159 50	
7.	Home computer	467 99	389 99	
8.	AM-FM radio	67 63	57 80	
9.	Table lamp	88 15	76 65	
10.	Exercise bicycle	102 50	93 49	
11.	Electric timer	45 00	39 95	
12.	Brass headboard	159 84	129 95	
13.	Computer desk	74 95	62 50	
14.	Recliner chair	477 95	419 25	
15.	Bedroom end table	108 55	88 98	
16.	Bathroom scale	67 70	56 42	
17.	Loveseat	413 97	369 95	
18.	Portable stereo	287 07	242 25	
19.	Coffee maker	57 00	49 95	
20.	Cordless telephone	78 94	65 50	

Exercise 13: Bank Deposits and Checks

To avoid overdrawing a checking account, you must keep a record of all deposits made and all checks issued. This is done in the register of the checkbook. When a deposit is made, the amount is entered in the register and added to the previous balance. Likewise, when a check is written, the amount is written in the register and subtracted from the previous balance. The last balance is the amount still on deposit.

In this exercise, the register has been abbreviated. The date, the name of the person to whom the check was issued, and the purpose of payment have been omitted. As one error will make the balances thereafter incorrect, strive for absolute accuracy. Be sure to subtract each check from the previous balance and to add each deposit.

BASIC TIME — 4 Minutes *(Estimated time to obtain a basic score of 100)*

Fill in the balances: (8 each)

Deposit	7,500.00
Check #1	387.40
Balance	
Check #2	45.37
Balance	
Check #3	125.75
Balance	
Deposit	275.43
Balance	
Check #4	18.70
Balance	
Check #5	12.50
Balance	
Check #6	3.48
Balance	
Deposit	134.29
Balance	
Check #7	217.65
Balance	
Check #8	91.34
Balance	
Check #9	13.60
Balance	
Deposit	418.50
Balance	
Check #10	137.50
Balance forward	

Balance for'd	
Check #11	51.35
Balance	
Check #12	33.87
Balance	
Deposit	218.75
Balance	
Check #13	10.15
Balance	
Check #14	72.83
Balance	
Check #15	27.92
Balance	
Check #16	84.27
Balance	
Deposit	135.20
Balance	
Check #17	72.60
Balance	
Check #18	49.38
Balance	
Check #19	138.96
Balance	
Deposit	187.50
Balance	

Test 13

Name _____
Date _____
Basic Time — 4 Minutes

Total Score _____
Basic Score   100
Improvement Score _____

Fill in the balances: (8 each)

Deposit	1,250	00	Balance for'd		
Check #1	38	75	Check #11	73	15
Balance			Balance		
Check #2	76	58	Check #12	47	84
Balance			Balance		
Check #3	135	63	Deposit	283	45
Balance			Balance		
Deposit	241	60	Check #13	68	46
Balance			Balance		
Check #4	62	15	Check #14	35	15
Balance			Balance		
Check #5	18	70	Check #15	75	23
Balance			Balance		
Check #6	47	25	Check #16	24	25
Balance			Balance		
Check #7	358	98	Deposit	126	50
Balance			Balance		
Deposit	139	50	Check #17	58	00
Balance			Balance		
Check #8	85	75	Check #18	27	18
Balance			Balance		
Check #9	92	32	Check #19	59	27
Balance			Balance		
Check #10	140	68	Deposit	46	35
Balance			Balance		
Deposit	256	35			
Balance forward					

Exercise 14: Customers' Accounts (Accounts Receivable)

This exercise illustrates one more practical use for your ability to add and subtract accurately and speedily. Here is a group of customers' accounts, or **accounts receivable**. An *account* is a ruled form in which amounts are recorded in a systematic manner. To save space here, only the money columns are shown; date and explanation columns are omitted.

In the first column headed Debit, charges made by the customer are written. In the second column headed Credit, payments on account are recorded. After every entry, the new account balance is shown in the third column. A debit amount is added to the previous balance in a customer's account. A credit amount is subtracted from the previous balance.

BASIC TIME — 5 Minutes *(Estimated time to obtain a basic score of 100)*

Find the balance after each debit or credit: (5 each)

1. Helen Herbert

DEBIT	CREDIT	BALANCE
44 19		44 19
132 22		
	100 00	
50 49		
	44 19	
	32 22	

2. Kathy Brightman

DEBIT	CREDIT	BALANCE
204 49		204 49
	150 00	
36 67		
	54 49	
109 19		
	100 00	

3. Hart & Cummings

DEBIT	CREDIT	BALANCE
345 19		345 19
	24 35	
152 15		
	320 84	
	100 00	
67 97		

4. Ana Guerra

DEBIT	CREDIT	BALANCE
78 09		78 09
	50 00	
96 76		
	3 48	
	28 09	
39 72		

5. William F. McCoy

DEBIT	CREDIT	BALANCE
135 05		135 05
	27 50	
	100 00	
19 95		
21 45		
36 59		
	50 00	
75 65		

6. The American Supply Co.

DEBIT	CREDIT	BALANCE
1,111 78		1,111 78
21 18		
	1,000 00	
50 43		

7. Lois Stein

DEBIT	CREDIT	BALANCE
24 72		24 72
	4 50	
	20 22	
92 41		

8. Brown-Seely Corporation

DEBIT	CREDIT	BALANCE
65 05		65 05
116 56		
92 41		
	65 05	
431 08		
	116 56	
301 44		
	250 00	

Test 14

Name _____   Total Score _____

Date _____   Basic Score **100**

Basic Time — 5 Minutes   Improvement Score _____

Find the new balance after each debit or credit entry. Remember that in a customer's account a debit is added to and a credit is subtracted from the previous balance. (5 each)

1. Ruby North

DEBIT	CREDIT	BALANCE
34 09		34 09
	4 04	
	30 05	
66 19		
39 47		

2. Marie Perez

DEBIT	CREDIT	BALANCE
44 06		44 06
100 67		
	44 06	
	100 67	
30 34		

3. Peterson Brothers

DEBIT	CREDIT	BALANCE
34 11		34 11
	7 17	
62 91		
	26 94	
32 22		
64 71		

4. Lawrence & Roche

DEBIT	CREDIT	BALANCE
38 21		38 21
	5 20	
64 44		
	33 01	
401 72		
	64 44	
	400 00	
129 09		

5. Ginger Spangler

DEBIT	CREDIT	BALANCE
67 72		67 72
304 11		
	150 00	
	75 00	
88 94		

6. J. F. McArthy & Sons

DEBIT	CREDIT	BALANCE
78 19		78 19
	2 27	
66 72		
34 01		
	100 00	

7. H. G. Fischer & Company

DEBIT	CREDIT	BALANCE
107 67		107 67
	100 00	
44 04		
32 96		
	7 67	
	50 00	

8. Debra Sidlowski

DEBIT	CREDIT	BALANCE
138 44		138 44
	100 00	
62 11		
46 51		
	38 44	
107 72		
29 89		
	150 00	

Exercise 15 — Application Problems

Both addition and subtraction are used in solving the problems in this exercise. Before starting to solve a word problem, carefully decide which operation is to be used.

Example A

Mr. Lerner earns $16,400 a year while Mrs. Lerner earns $22,600 a year. What is their total income?

$16,400 + $22,600 = $39,000

Example B

How much more does Mrs. Lerner earn than Mr. Lerner?

$22,600 − $16,400 = $6,200 more

BASIC TIME — 7 Minutes (Estimated time to obtain a basic score of 100)

Solve these problems. Write the answers in the spaces on the right. (20 each)

1. An automobile salesman will allow Tom Gartner a trade-in allowance of $3,865 toward the purchase of a new car priced at $10,749. How much difference will Tom have to pay in order to buy the new car? .... _____

2. In West City there were two big games on the same day. At the football game there were 47,117 people; at the baseball game, 62,122. How many more people attended the baseball game than attended the football game? .... _____

3. A hiker carried a tent weighing 7 pounds, a pack weighing 38 pounds, and a sleeping bag weighing 4 pounds. How much weight did the hiker carry? .... _____

4. On January 1 Alice Mukuda's automobile mileage reading was 10,846. On December 31 the reading was 39,367. How many miles was Alice's automobile driven during the year? .... _____

5. An automobile dealer sold 7 cars on Monday, 6 on Tuesday, 8 on Wednesday, 13 on Thursday, 24 on Friday, and 9 on Saturday. How many automobiles were sold during these six days? .... _____

6. At the beginning of the week, a gasoline pump showed a reading of 27,366. At the end of the week, the gasoline pump meter showed 40,887. According to the meter, how many gallons of gasoline were sold through this pump during the week? .... _____

7. In the first of three offices, there were 32 desks, in the second, 26; and in the third, 41. How many desks were in the three offices? .... _____

8. The population of Kenton is 13,587 and of Corinth 70,137. By how much is the population of Corinth greater than that of Kenton? .... _____

9. How many gallons of gasoline can be refined from a 42-gallon barrel of crude oil which also yields the following: 20 gallons of fuel oil, 4 gallons of kerosene, 2 gallons of lubricating oil, 3 gallons of miscellaneous products, and 2 gallons of waste? .... _____

10. A 17-foot canoe will support 650 pounds without sinking. If it were occupied by three persons weighing 130 pounds, 203 pounds, and 196 pounds, how much more weight should it hold without sinking? .... _____

Test 15

Name _____ Total Score _____

Date _____ Basic Score   100

Basic Time — 5 Minutes   Improvement Score _____

Solve these problems. Write the answers in the spaces on the right. (20 each)

1. A baker needed 626 pounds of materials to produce 548 pounds of bread. What is the difference between the total weight of the materials and the total weight of the bread? .... _____

2. A nurse at City General Hospital counted 17 beds in one ward, 28 in another, and 39 in a third. How many beds did the nurse count in these wards? .... _____

3. A camper was driven 247 miles the first day and 151 miles the second day. How many miles was it driven in these two days? .... _____

4. If the mileage reading of an automobile was 26,970 at the beginning of the day and 27,249 at the end of the day, how many miles was the automobile driven that day? .... _____

5. An-Ping Shen paid $63 for her automobile license, $3,580 income tax, and $1,795 property tax. What was her total expenditure for these items? .... _____

6. The area of Alaska is 586,400 square miles. The area of Texas is 267,339 square miles. In square miles, how much larger is Alaska than Texas? .... _____

7. The Jennings Manufacturing Company has liabilities totaling $597,592 and assets amounting to $904,325. By how much do the assets exceed the liabilities? _____

8. During one week, a delivery truck was driven 42 miles on Monday, 78 miles on Tuesday, 36 miles on Wednesday, 91 miles on Thursday, 74 miles on Friday, and 37 miles on Saturday. How many miles was the truck driven that week? .... _____

9. Graton Community College requires 62 semester units for graduation with an Associate Arts degree. If Steve Magosci has earned 16, 17, and 14 units during his three semesters at the college, how many units must he earn his fourth semester in order to graduate? .... _____

10. At the beginning of November, the balance in a checking account was $784. During the month, checks for $39, $136, $18, $247, and $52 were written. Find the balance after these checks were deducted. .... _____

Exercise 16 — Multiplication, 196 Key Combinations

Multiplication is the third basic operation in mathematics. It is a shortcut method of addition. For example, if you correctly add four 3's, the result will be 12 — the same as 3 multiplied by 4. The top (or first) number is called the **multiplicand**; the bottom (or second) number is called the **multiplier**; the result of multiplication is called the **product**. See the example at the right. Learn thoroughly the multiplication tables from 2 through 15.

In the form below, there are spaces for the products of 196 combinations in multiplication. You are to write these products in the spaces. Each square is to be filled in with the product that is the result of multiplying the number in the top row by the number in the left column.

```
   3
   3     3 multiplicand
   3    ×4 multiplier
   3    12 product
  ---
  12
```

BASIC TIME — 4 Minutes *(Estimated time to obtain a basic score of 100)*

Write the products in the squares as indicated: (1 each, 196 points)

	a	b	c	d	e	f	g	h	i	j	k	l	m	n
	1	2	3	4	5	6	7	8	9	10	11	12	13	14	15
1.	2														
2.	3														
3.	4														
4.	5														
5.	6														
6.	7														
7.	8														
8.	9														
9.	10|													
10.	11														
11.	12														
12.	13														
13.	14														
14.	15														

Test 16

Name _____
Date _____
Basic Time — 3 Minutes

Total Score _____
Basic Score __100__
Improvement Score _____

Write products in squares as in the preceding exercise: (2 each)

	a	b	c	d	e	f	g	h	i	j
	6	15	11	7	14	9	12	8	13	5
1.	4									
2.	14									
3.	9									
4.	12									
5.	8									
6.	11									
7.	6									
8.	15									
9.	7									
10.	13									

Exercise 17: Multiplication with One-Digit Multipliers

Multiplying by 2, 3, 4, and 5 is often easier than multiplying by 6, 7, 8, and 9. If the multiplication facts have been thoroughly memorized, however, even these latter digits will present little, if any, difficulty.

At times you must carry numerals. You may write down the carry numerals as shown in the example at the right, or simply remember them. Use the method that works better for you. In the example, 28 is multiplied by 7. The carry numeral is 5.

Solution. (1) Multiply 8 (ones) by 7 to obtain 56 (ones). Write 6 below the 7 in the ones place and carry the 5 (tens).

```
   5
  28    ( 2 tens + 8 ones)
  ×7    (         ×7       )
 ───    ─────────────────
 196    (14 tens + 56 ones)
```

(2) Multiply 2 (tens) by 7 to obtain 14 (tens). To the 14 (tens), add the carried 5 (tens) to obtain 19 (tens). Write 9 in the tens place and 1 in the hundreds place. The product is 196.

BASIC TIME — 8 Minutes (Estimated time to obtain a basic score of 100)

Multiply: (2 each)

	a	b	c	d	e	f	g	h	i	j
1.	52 ×2	21 ×3	33 ×4	22 ×5	54 ×2	43 ×3	53 ×4	62 ×5	63 ×4	92 ×3
2.	44 ×2	34 ×3	35 ×2	43 ×2	52 ×6	53 ×2	41 ×7	55 ×2	62 ×8	74 ×3
3.	73 ×8	64 ×8	42 ×5	84 ×3	45 ×7	52 ×8	53 ×4	84 ×6	54 ×4	64 ×3
4.	56 ×5	65 ×4	64 ×9	66 ×7	74 ×8	72 ×6	77 ×4	62 ×7	86 ×8	28 ×6
5.	87 ×5	84 ×7	88 ×8	94 ×8	99 ×6	98 ×9	78 ×5	86 ×6	93 ×8	96 ×7
6.	90 ×8	92 ×9	94 ×5	87 ×6	99 ×7	99 ×8	82 ×8	32 ×6	79 ×7	50 ×9
7.	52 ×9	83 ×6	94 ×7	82 ×7	65 ×9	52 ×7	35 ×9	93 ×7	88 ×7	77 ×8
8.	93 ×6	98 ×7	95 ×9	75 ×7	96 ×8	48 ×7	96 ×6	54 ×8	87 ×7	60 ×9
9.	95 ×7	96 ×9	98 ×8	97 ×8	79 ×9	91 ×8	86 ×7	92 ×6	89 ×8	87 ×9
10.	79 ×8	85 ×8	93 ×9	99 ×9	97 ×9	98 ×6	87 ×8	78 ×7	68 ×8	94 ×9

Test 17

Name _____   Total Score _____
Date _____   Basic Score   100
Basic Time — 7 Minutes   Improvement Score _____

Multiply: (2 each)

	a	b	c	d	e	f	g	h	i	j
1.	52 × 3	82 × 7	62 × 2	32 × 8	92 × 4	42 × 8	72 × 9	91 × 6	92 × 5	31 × 9
2.	63 × 6	93 × 4	93 × 8	43 × 9	83 × 7	41 × 5	95 × 4	45 × 7	44 × 9	47 × 6
3.	53 × 9	56 × 8	59 × 7	60 × 5	54 × 9	67 × 7	65 × 6	68 × 6	69 × 7	62 × 9
4.	78 × 8	72 × 6	84 × 6	77 × 8	78 × 7	85 × 8	89 × 7	86 × 6	88 × 9	87 × 8
5.	94 × 7	98 × 7	99 × 6	95 × 7	92 × 6	97 × 8	94 × 6	93 × 9	90 × 8	96 × 9
6.	22 × 9	32 × 7	97 × 6	99 × 7	84 × 9	92 × 8	63 × 9	89 × 8	66 × 7	69 × 8
7.	88 × 7	44 × 8	86 × 7	84 × 8	94 × 8	70 × 8	78 × 8	75 × 7	85 × 9	86 × 9
8.	73 × 7	75 × 8	76 × 9	97 × 7	82 × 9	87 × 6	85 × 8	88 × 8	90 × 6	98 × 8
9.	93 × 6	96 × 8	97 × 9	98 × 9	92 × 7	95 × 9	83 × 6	86 × 8	89 × 7	99 × 8
10.	99 × 5	98 × 5	89 × 9	78 × 6	69 × 9	79 × 8	96 × 6	99 × 9	79 × 7	98 × 6

Exercise 18 — Multiplication with Two- and Three-Digit Multipliers

When multiplying by a number that contains two or more digits, you must be careful to align the partial products properly. The right-hand digit of each partial product is written directly below the multiplying digit. This causes the partial products to be properly aligned so that tens will be added to tens, hundreds to hundreds, etc. The partial products are added together to obtain the final product, as shown in the example at the right.

```
    5,746   multiplicand
   × 312   multiplier
   11 492  first partial product
   57 46   second partial product
  1 723 8  third partial product
  1,792,752 product
```

BASIC TIME — 15 Minutes *(Estimated time to obtain a basic score of 100)*

Multiply and insert commas in the product where applicable:

	a	b	c	d	e	f	g	h	
1.	34 × 22	37 × 12	42 × 21	54 × 32	45 × 21	43 × 22	45 × 12	46 × 23	(4)
2.	95 × 29	69 × 26	98 × 21	89 × 23	81 × 27	99 × 32	98 × 37	95 × 23	(4)
3.	82 × 47	79 × 43	59 × 47	87 × 42	86 × 55	67 × 24	74 × 31	97 × 84	(4)

	a	b	c	d	e	f	
4.	798 × 54	938 × 64	786 × 35	587 × 57	241 × 36	351 × 78	(6)
5.	651 × 88	597 × 27	489 × 36	792 × 91	563 × 99	938 × 35	(6)

	a	b	c	d	
6.	7,864 × 381	8,955 × 275	8,926 × 698	6,847 × 457	(8)

Test 18

Name _____ Total Score _____

Date _____ Basic Score **100**

Basic Time — 12 Minutes Improvement Score _____

Multiply and insert commas in the product where applicable:

	a	b	c	d	e	f	g	h	
1.	63 × 32	46 × 23	95 × 21	42 × 31	73 × 34	93 × 43	85 × 12	94 × 23	(4)
2.	54 × 14	93 × 62	53 × 26	99 × 23	92 × 62	83 × 39	69 × 13	86 × 26	(4)
3.	96 × 34	86 × 79	89 × 88	93 × 29	84 × 35	78 × 46	98 × 79	97 × 57	(4)

	a	b	c	d	e	f	
4.	573 × 35	388 × 54	676 × 96	826 × 87	976 × 63	778 × 77	(6)
5.	854 × 37	957 × 84	575 × 53	597 × 79	978 × 69	978 × 99	(6)

	a	b	c	d	
6.	3,914 × 573	9,833 × 452	7,256 × 769	9,342 × 684	(8)

Exercise 19: Multiplication with 0 in Multiplicand and in Multiplier

Zeros often cause errors in multiplication. Some people make errors when 0 is in a multiplication problem because (1) they forget that 0 multiplied by any number always equals 0, and (2) they carelessly misplace numerals in partial products.

For example, 4 × 0 simply means 0 + 0 + 0 + 0. This equals 0. Reversing the numerals in the problem gives 0 × 4, which means "not any" 4's. Zero is merely the symbol used to represent none. You can avoid having difficulty with 0's in multiplication if you will remember (1) zero means "not any," and (2) the right-hand digit of each partial product is placed directly below its multiplying digit.

The example below shows two ways of multiplying by zero. The second method is shorter and more commonly used.

```
    3,405
   ×2,001                    3,405
    3 405                   ×2,001
   00 00        or           3 405
  000 0                     6 810 00
  6 810                     6,813,405
  6,813,405
```

BASIC TIME — 8 Minutes *(Estimated time to obtain a basic score of 100)*

Multiply and insert commas in the product:

	a	b	c	d	e
1.	3,002 9	5,006 8	4,007 7	6,008 6	7,009 5 (4)
2.	304 31	502 23	605 45	309 67	708 89 (6)
3.	4,003 87	5,006 79	7,005 78	8,090 67	9,070 86 (8)
4.	712 304	322 406	793 507	754 608	919 809 (10)
5.	6,400 6,005	7,500 8,090	4,030 7,040	7,809 9,060	8,069 7,004 (12)

Test 19

40

Name _____
Date _____
Basic Time — 10 Minutes

Total Score _____
Basic Score   100
Improvement Score _____

Multiply and insert commas in the product:

	a	b	c	d	e	
1.	3,010 × 5	4,006 × 6	5,090 × 7	6,100 × 8	7,055 × 9	(4)
2.	907 × 28	908 × 37	804 × 45	806 × 56	604 × 79	(6)
3.	3,002 × 59	5,008 × 68	4,007 × 76	9,050 × 85	8,060 × 94	(8)
4.	688 × 707	775 × 608	632 × 508	849 × 409	609 × 509	(10)
5.	6,500 × 5,060	9,507 × 7,005	8,070 × 8,040	8,700 × 8,600	7,084 × 8,900	(12)

Exercise 20: Checking Multiplication by Casting Out 9's

The remainder obtained when a number is divided by 9 is the **excess of 9's** in that number. Notice that 23 ÷ 9 = 2 with a remainder of 5. The excess of 9's in the number 23 is 5, which may be obtained quickly by adding the digits (2 + 3) that are in the number. The excess of 9's in any number may be obtained by the addition of the digits. **Casting out 9's** is the procedure of finding the excess of 9's in a number.

A quick check on the accuracy of the product of a long multiplication problem can be performed by casting out 9's. In order to prove the accuracy of a product by casting out 9's, follow these steps: (1) Determine the excess of 9's in the multiplicand and in the multiplier by adding the digits in each. (Add results until one digit is obtained for each number.) (2) Multiply these excesses to obtain the product of the excesses. (3) Determine the excess of 9's in the product of the excesses. (4) Determine the excess of 9's in the product of the problem. The check number obtained in Step 3 must equal the check number obtained in Step 4.

In short, the multiplication is presumed to be accurate when the excess of 9's in the product of the excesses equals the excess of 9's in the product of the problem.

Check

```
 2,437  →   7 excess of 9's in multiplicand
×  165  →  ×3 excess of 9's in multiplier
 12 185    21 product of excesses
 146 22     3 excess of 9's in product of excesses
 243 7           equals
402,105 →   3 excess of 9's in product
```

BASIC TIME — 15 Minutes *(Estimated time to obtain a basic score of 100)*

Multiply, insert commas in the product, and check your answer by casting out 9's:

	a	b	c	d
1.	548 × 32	405 × 87	728 × 64	840 × 50

Check No. _____   Check No. _____   Check No. _____   Check No. _____ (4)

(10)

	a	b	c
2.	65,215 × 3,065	73,271 × 3,404	92,070 × 3,602

Check No. _____   Check No. _____   Check No. _____ (5)

(17)

3.	9,879 × 2,716	63,695 × 23,740	99,301 × 46,263

Check No. _____   Check No. _____   Check No. _____ (6)

(20)

Test 20

Name _____ Total Score _____

Date _____ Basic Score __100__

Basic Time — 15 Minutes Improvement Score _____

Multiply, insert commas in the product, and check your answer by casting out 9's:

	a Check	b Check	c Check	d Check	
1.	208 51	824 65	797 35	801 48	(8)
	Check No. ____	Check No. ____	Check No. ____	Check No. ____	(2)

	a Check	b Check	c Check	
2.	6,123 327	3,602 376	7,028 287	(12)
	Check No. ____	Check No. ____	Check No. ____	(4)

	a Check	b Check	c Check	
3.	75,460 4,243	10,207 4,529	48,255 9,146	(16)
	Check No. ____	Check No. ____	Check No. ____	(4)

	a Check	b Check	
4.	50,182 46,854	97,864 83,032	(20)
	Check No. ____	Check No. ____	(6)

Exercise 21: Multiplication by 10 and by Multiples of 10

Numbers ending in zero present the greatest possibilities for shortcuts in multiplication. Study the shortcuts listed below until you know them thoroughly.

To multiply any number by 10, simply add a 0 to the right of the number.

To multiply any number by 20, multiply the number by 2 and add a 0 to the right of the result.

To multiply any number by 30, multiply the number by 3 and add a 0 to the right of the result.

Mentally complete the above set of rules through 40, 50, 60, 70, 80 and 90.

To multiply any number by 100, add two 0's to the right of the number.

To multiply any number by 200, multiply the number by 2 and add two 0's to the right of the result. See the example at the right.

```
   63
  200
------
12,600
```

Mentally complete the above set of rules through 900.

To multiply any number by 1,000, add three 0's to the right of the number.

To multiply any number by 2,000, multiply the number by 2 and add three 0's to the right of the result.

Mentally complete the above set of rules through 9,000.

BASIC TIME — 4 Minutes *(Estimated time to obtain a basic score of 100)*

Multiply and insert commas in the product where applicable: (2 each)

	a	b	c	d
1.	63 × 10 =	98 × 9,000 =	51 × 7,000 =	135 × 10 =
2.	63 × 100 =	56 × 10 =	53 × 8,000 =	254 × 100 =
3.	63 × 1,000 =	87 × 100 =	57 × 9,000 =	362 × 1,000 =
4.	63 × 30 =	92 × 1,000 =	59 × 10 =	451 × 20 =
5.	63 × 40 =	14 × 20 =	61 × 20 =	532 × 30 =
6.	63 × 50 =	16 × 30 =	63 × 30 =	617 × 40 =
7.	63 × 60 =	17 × 40 =	65 × 40 =	781 × 50 =
8.	63 × 70 =	18 × 50 =	67 × 50 =	893 × 60 =
9.	63 × 80 =	19 × 60 =	69 × 60 =	918 × 70 =
10.	63 × 90 =	21 × 70 =	71 × 70 =	122 × 80 =
11.	63 × 200 =	22 × 80 =	73 × 80 =	266 × 90 =
12.	63 × 300 =	23 × 90 =	75 × 90 =	345 × 200 =
13.	63 × 400 =	32 × 200 =	76 × 100 =	456 × 300 =
14.	63 × 500 =	33 × 300 =	77 × 200 =	576 × 400 =
15.	63 × 600 =	35 × 400 =	79 × 300 =	677 × 500 =
16.	63 × 700 =	37 × 500 =	81 × 400 =	789 × 600 =
17.	63 × 800 =	39 × 600 =	83 × 500 =	803 × 700 =
18.	63 × 900 =	41 × 700 =	85 × 600 =	904 × 800 =
19.	98 × 2,000 =	43 × 800 =	87 × 700 =	994 × 900 =
20.	98 × 3,000 =	45 × 900 =	89 × 800 =	102 × 2,000 =
21.	98 × 4,000 =	47 × 2,000 =	91 × 900 =	117 × 3,000 =
22.	98 × 5,000 =	47 × 3,000 =	16 × 20 =	124 × 4,000 =
23.	98 × 6,000 =	47 × 4,000 =	23 × 30 =	137 × 5,000 =
24.	98 × 7,000 =	47 × 5,000 =	34 × 40 =	242 × 6,000 =
25.	98 × 8,000 =	49 × 6,000 =	35 × 60 =	999 × 7,000 =

Test 21

Name _____ Total Score _____
Date _____ Basic Score   100
Basic Time — 3 Minutes   Improvement Score _____

Multiply and insert commas in the product where applicable: (2 each)

	a	b	c	d
1.	16 × 10 = _____	104 × 1,000 = _____	22 × 10 = _____	195 × 200 = _____
2.	61 × 10 = _____	114 × 2,000 = _____	32 × 10 = _____	185 × 300 = _____
3.	17 × 100 = _____	124 × 3,000 = _____	42 × 20 = _____	989 × 800 = _____
4.	71 × 100 = _____	132 × 4,000 = _____	52 × 30 = _____	978 × 600 = _____
5.	18 × 1,000 = _____	133 × 5,000 = _____	62 × 30 = _____	884 × 700 = _____
6.	81 × 1,000 = _____	234 × 6,000 = _____	72 × 40 = _____	884 × 900 = _____
7.	19 × 20 = _____	235 × 7,000 = _____	72 × 50 = _____	848 × 800 = _____
8.	91 × 200 = _____	346 × 8,000 = _____	72 × 60 = _____	777 × 700 = _____
9.	21 × 300 = _____	413 × 9,000 = _____	72 × 70 = _____	677 × 800 = _____
10.	32 × 400 = _____	556 × 10 = _____	83 × 80 = _____	553 × 300 = _____
11.	23 × 500 = _____	671 × 100 = _____	84 × 90 = _____	456 × 400 = _____
12.	34 × 600 = _____	819 × 20 = _____	94 × 100 = _____	465 × 400 = _____
13.	43 × 700 = _____	818 × 200 = _____	94 × 1,000 = _____	564 × 500 = _____
14.	45 × 800 = _____	944 × 30 = _____	49 × 20 = _____	546 × 600 = _____
15.	54 × 900 = _____	112 × 20 = _____	94 × 30 = _____	674 × 700 = _____
16.	56 × 2,000 = _____	174 × 20 = _____	89 × 90 = _____	687 × 900 = _____
17.	65 × 3,000 = _____	184 × 30 = _____	98 × 80 = _____	781 × 800 = _____
18.	67 × 4,000 = _____	148 × 40 = _____	77 × 10 = _____	780 × 800 = _____
19.	76 × 5,000 = _____	184 × 60 = _____	77 × 1,000 = _____	345 × 800 = _____
20.	68 × 6,000 = _____	214 × 70 = _____	89 × 40 = _____	354 × 200 = _____
21.	86 × 7,000 = _____	412 × 80 = _____	98 × 4,000 = _____	516 × 400 = _____
22.	79 × 8,000 = _____	516 × 90 = _____	76 × 3,000 = _____	561 × 500 = _____
23.	97 × 9,000 = _____	516 × 900 = _____	23 × 300 = _____	324 × 600 = _____
24.	98 × 20 = _____	723 × 10 = _____	49 × 200 = _____	342 × 700 = _____
25.	97 × 300 = _____	132 × 30 = _____	78 × 90 = _____	324 × 7,000 = _____

Exercise 22 Application Problems

These word problems require addition, subtraction, and multiplication facts. Carefully decide which operation is needed before solving the problems below.

> **Example**
> A college student reads on the average 300 pages a week. If a term last 15 weeks, how many pages does this student read in one term?
>
> 300 × 15 = 4,500 pages

BASIC TIME — 8 Minutes *(Estimated time to obtain a basic score of 100)*

Solve these problems. Write the answers in the spaces on the right. (20 each)

1. The deputy sheriff had the following scores in target practice: 9, 7, 8, 9, 6, 10, 7, 9. What was the total score? ....

2. The bituminous coal from Franklin County, Illinois, has an average heat value (British Thermal Units) per pound of 11,930. Lignite coal from Houston County, Texas, has an average of 7,140 BTU's per pound. This is a difference of how many BTU's per pound? ....

3. How much weight is handled by a person who moves 657 boxes of apples if each box weighs 60 pounds? ....

4. Two herds of cattle were counted. The first contained 47 steers; the second, 56. How many steers were in these two herds? ....

5. At the beginning of the year, there were 68,809 people registered at the state unemployment office and 53,910 registered at the end of the year. This is a decrease of how many? ....

6. If a bakery sold an average of 904 cakes a day, how many cakes would it sell in a month in which it was open 27 days? ....

7. If a person can type at an average speed of 64 words a minute, how many words can be typed in 42 minutes? ....

8. How far can a truck travel on 98 gallons of gasoline if it averages 13 miles to a gallon? ....

9. The average attendance at the Strand Theater was 753 people for 468 consecutive performances. How many people attended during this period of time? ....

10. In a new subdivision of Eaglespoint, there are 86 condominiums worth $139,725 each. What is the total value of these condominiums? ....

Test 22

Name _____ Total Score _____

Date _____ Basic Score ____100____

Basic Time — 7 Minutes Improvement Score _____

Solve these problems. Write the answers in the spaces on the right. (20 each)

1. The Wyoming Hikers Club walked 28 miles on Thursday, 27 miles on Friday, and 26 miles on Saturday. How many total miles did the club hike on Friday and Saturday? .... _____

2. A small airplane flies at an average ground speed of 158 miles an hour. How far will it travel in 17 hours? .... _____

3. Figure the difference if the subtrahend is 1,051 and the minuend is 1,958. .... _____

4. Last year Argon Taxi Service bought 63 new taxicabs at $13,798 each. What was the total cost? .... _____

5. The demand for electric motors caused Universal Motors to deplete its stock and to ship the motors as fast as they were produced. During this time the company produced an average of 1,867 motors every day for 34 days. What is the total number of motors shipped during this period? .... _____

6. The Alert Answering Service handled 639 messages a day during February (28 days). What was the total number of messages handled for this month? .... _____

7. The most expensive section of a highway cost two million dollars a mile for 92 miles. What was the total cost of constructing this section? .... _____

8. For the spring semester, 2,314 freshmen and 1,740 sophomores were enrolled at Denton University. What was the total enrollment for these two classes? .... _____

9. A new office center contains 19 offices of 950 square feet each, 25 offices of 1,200 square feet each, and 9 offices of 1,500 square feet each. This center contains how many square feet of office space? .... _____

10. A building being constructed is to have 376 windows. Each window is to contain 18 panes of glass. How many panes of glass will be needed? .... _____

Exercise 23 — Division Facts

Division is the fourth and last basic operation in mathematics. It is the process of finding how many times one number can be contained in another. In effect, division is the inverse (opposite) of multiplication. The number to be divided is the **dividend**; the number that does the dividing is the **divisor**; the result obtained by division is the **quotient**. To prove the quotient, multiply the divisor by the quotient to get the dividend.

See the example at the right. If 6 is divided by 2, the quotient is 3. Then to prove the answer, multiply the divisor 2 by the quotient 3 to get the dividend 6.

$$\text{divisor } 2 \overline{\smash{\big)}\, 6} \text{ dividend} \quad \text{(3 quotient)}$$

This exercise contains the 90 basic division facts arranged in random order. Since division is closely related to multiplication, a review of the multiplication tables will prove helpful. Before writing the quotients, do them mentally until you can complete them accurately in one minute. Then time yourself as you write the quotients. Test 23 may then be used as a speed test.

BASIC TIME — 1 Minute *(Estimated time to obtain a basic score of 100)*

Divide: (2 each, 180 points)

	a	b	c	d	e	f	g	h	i
1.	4)0	5)5	7)0	1)4	1)8	2)4	9)9	6)0	1)3
2.	3)6	8)16	9)27	8)0	2)0	6)12	8)48	4)24	8)40
3.	7)42	9)45	2)10	1)6	8)64	4)32	9)54	6)6	2)6
4.	4)16	8)8	1)0	6)30	5)45	2)16	9)81	9)18	8)72
5.	5)10	7)21	1)7	9)63	7)56	9)36	8)32	4)36	9)0
6.	3)24	4)8	2)2	5)0	3)18	2)14	8)56	2)18	4)20
7.	5)20	7)35	6)36	1)9	7)63	6)48	5)30	3)27	5)40
8.	4)12	9)72	3)3	7)7	6)24	6)18	2)12	3)0	4)28
9.	5)15	7)28	7)14	5)25	3)21	6)54	1)5	3)15	6)42
10.	5)35	3)12	3)9	7)49	4)4	8)24	2)8	1)2	1)1

Test 23

Name _____ Total Score _____
Date _____ Basic Score   80
Basic Time — 1 Minute   Improvement Score _____

Divide: (2 each, 180 points)

	a	b	c	d	e	f	g	h	i
1.	1)5	2)8	7)0	9)9	4)0	1)8	3)9	2)4	4)4
2.	8)8	5)10	8)24	7)63	2)10	3)12	1)9	3)27	1)1
3.	4)24	4)16	8)72	4)32	2)12	5)45	7)7	1)7	6)6
4.	7)21	7)42	9)0	9)36	7)35	7)56	5)25	3)15	3)21
5.	7)49	4)20	9)45	7)28	1)0	8)0	9)27	8)48	6)12
6.	8)32	5)40	5)15	2)14	7)14	1)6	2)16	9)54	9)18
7.	6)24	4)28	4)12	6)48	1)3	5)35	8)40	6)30	4)36
8.	8)16	5)5	5)20	6)18	3)18	9)81	8)64	9)63	2)18
9.	8)56	6)42	3)24	6)54	9)72	6)36	5)30	5)0	3)0
10.	2)6	1)4	4)8	1)2	2)2	2)0	3)3	6)0	3)6

Exercise 24 — Division with Small Divisors

This exercise is limited to division by numbers up to and including 12. The method to be used here is known as **short division**. Only the quotients are to be written.

Start dividing on the left. If you like, write each "carryover" digit as a small numeral to the left of the next digit. Show any remainder in parentheses to the right of the quotient. See the example at the right.

Solution. As 10 contains two 5's, write 2 over the 0. The 8 contains one 5 with 3 "left over," so write 1 over the 8, and carry 3 to the left of the 9. As 39 contains 7 fives with 4 remaining, write 7 over the 9. Show the remainder, 4, in parentheses next to the quotient.

$$\begin{array}{r} 2\ 1\ 7\ (4) \\ 5\overline{)1{,}0\ 8^{3}9} \end{array}$$

BASIC TIME — 4 Minutes *(Estimated time to obtain a basic score of 100)*

Divide and show any remainder in parentheses next to the quotient: (198 points)

	a	b	c	
1.	2⟌8,423	3⟌6,373	4⟌8,497	(6)
2.	4⟌84,536	5⟌55,673	6⟌97,268	(6)
3.	7⟌77,950	8⟌69,208	9⟌11,106	(6)
4.	2⟌1,764,911	3⟌547,691	4⟌742,351	(6)
5.	5⟌173,855	6⟌284,156	7⟌932,617	(6)
6.	7⟌6,382,523	8⟌1,175,140	9⟌7,369,792	(10)
7.	10⟌154,110	11⟌57,388	12⟌25,816	(12)
8.	10⟌427,623	11⟌782,386	12⟌736,254	(14)

Test 24

Name _____ Total Score _____
Date _____ Basic Score ___98___
Basic Time — 4 Minutes   Improvement Score _____

Divide and show any remainder in parentheses next to the quotient: (198 points)

	a	b	c	
1.	2)6,742	3)9,427	4)1,478	(6)
2.	5)65,675	6)27,462	7)69,378	(6)
3.	6)26,948	8)36,278	9)19,314	(6)
4.	3)124,692	4)678,449	5)345,671	(6)
5.	6)673,272	7)114,431	8)753,834	(6)
6.	5)1,823,976	8)2,545,138	7)1,957,295	(10)
7.	10)261,180	11)129,096	12)145,729	(12)
8.	10)211,926	11)134,554	12)146,798	(14)

Exercise 25: Long Division

Long division is the name applied to division by numbers that cannot readily be used as simple divisors. The individual products and remainders, because of their length, are written down.

In the example at the right, 159,872 (the **dividend**) is divided by 364 (the **divisor**) to give a **quotient** of 439 and a **remainder** of 76.

Solution. First, 364 goes into 1598 four times with a remainder. Write 4 above the 8 of the dividend. Then multiply this 4 by the divisor of 364. Write your answer, 1456, under 1598, and subtract to find the remainder of 142.

Bring down the next digit 7 from the dividend to get 1427. Divide 1427 by 364 to get 3 plus a remainder. Write 3 above the 7 of the dividend, and multiply the 3 by the divisor of 364. The answer, 1092, is subtracted from 1427 to give 335.

Bring down the 2 from the dividend to get 3352. Divide 3352 by 364 to get 9 plus a remainder. Write 9 above the 2 of the dividend, and multiply by the divisor of 364. The answer, 3276, is subtracted from 3352 to give a remainder of 76.

```
            439
    364) 159,872
         145 6
          14 27
          10 92
           3 352
           3 276
              76
```

BASIC TIME — 6 Minutes *(Estimated time to obtain a basic score of 100)*

Divide: (198 points)

	a	b	c
1.	368) 49,307	374) 59,368	746) 83,549 (18)
2.	587) 90,294	845) 123,925	639) 101,623 (18)
3.	3,412) 51,709	9,063) 134,263	6,714) 84,627 (18)
4.	387) 12,463	596) 11,576	439) 12,590 (12)

Test 25

52

Name _____ Total Score _____
Date _____   Basic Score __100__
Basic Time — 5 Minutes   Improvement Score _____

Divide: (201 points)

	a	b	c	
1.	326)4,827	593)6,524	728)9,518	(13)
2.	928)10,693	851)16,275	627)8,276	(13)
3.	1,351)63,475	2,876)92,467	5,489)136,784	(17)
4.	529)72,673	865)163,724	7,563)2,037,865	(24)

Exercise 26 Zeros in the Quotient

When dividing, some people have difficulty in correctly placing 0's in the quotient. Because 0 serves as a place holder, an omitted 0 causes the quotient to be wrong.

If the number to be divided is smaller than the divisor after a digit is brought down from the dividend, a 0 must be placed in the quotient above that dividend digit.

Example A. After 18 is divided into 55 three times with a remainder of 1 and the 2 is brought down, the 12 is smaller than the 18. Therefore, write 0 above the 2, bring down the 6, and divide 18 into 126.

A division problem is not complete until a digit is placed in the quotient directly above the last digit in the dividend.

Example A

```
          307                    307
     18 ) 5,526             18 ) 5,526
          5 4                    5 4
           12        or           126
           00                     126
           126
           126
```

Example B. As the remainder 15 is smaller than the divisor 23, write 0 in the quotient above the 5.

Example B
```
         40
    23 ) 935
         92
          15
```

BASIC TIME — 10 Minutes *(Estimated time to obtain a basic score of 100)*

Divide and show any remainder in parentheses:

	a	b	c	
1.	6) 1,830	7) 1,442	9) 3,663	(10)
2.	8) 8,664	9) 6,309	7) 8,406	(10)
3.	14) 28,098	15) 45,315	19) 58,387	(14)
4.	45) 67,635	61) 128,466	74) 266,457	(18)

	a	b	
5.	82) 16,457,482	95) 66,528,880	(22)

Test 26

Name _____
Date _____
Basic Time — 8 Minutes

Total Score _____
Basic Score __100__
Improvement Score _____

Divide and show any remainder in parentheses:

   a   b   c

1. 16)4,880 23)9,361 34)27,268 (16)

2. 45)225,287 67)268,536 78)546,702 (18)

3. 86)776,580 92)372,682 97)682,977 (18)

   a   b

4. 403)8,181,606 473)14,228,786 (22)

Exercise 27 Finding Averages

This exercise provides practice in **averaging numbers**; that is, finding a number that is representative of all the numbers in a set.

To find the average of a set of numbers, add the numbers and then divide the sum by the number of numbers in the set.

Example. Find the average of these numbers:

28, 47, 63, 75

Solution. 1. Add the numbers.
2. Divide the sum by the number of numbers in the set.

Example

Step 1

```
   28
   47   (4 numbers
   63    in a set)
   75
  213
```

Step 2

$$4 \overline{)213} = 53\tfrac{1}{4} \text{ average}$$

```
     20
     13
     12
      1
```
(Place the remainder over the divisor as a fraction)

BASIC TIME — 8 Minutes *(Estimated time to obtain a basic score of 100)*

Find the average for each set of numbers. Show any remainder over the divisor as a fractional part.

1. 27, 38, 52, 69, 74 _____ (8)

2. 129, 76, 257, 342, 638, 221 _____ (22)

3. 543, 628, 947, 463, 296, 382, 543, 624 _____ (20)

4. 228, 469, 133, 546, 1,020, 314, 847 _____ (16)

5. 36, 73, 56, 85, 92, 43, 61, 28, 73, 57, 42, 38, 31 _____ (20)

6. The number of customers on consecutive days were as follows:

    296, 305, 326, 321, 310, 342, 356, 332, 363

    Find the average number of customers per day.............................. _____ (20)

7. The individual weights of a soccer team were:

    204, 196, 189, 184, 176, 167, 164, 163, 160, 151, 145

    What was the average weight?.. _____ (24)

8. Find the average of the following daily sales:

    $211,768; $196,725; $205,689; $225,983; $189,658; $254,879 .... _____ (34)

9. Find the average daily school attendance:

    1,479; 1,498; 1,505; 1,512; 1,463 .... _____ (14)

10. Find the average of the following daily attendance at basketball games:

    7,825; 2,649; 5,684; 6,392; 3,476; 4,368; 2,556; 5,275 .... _____ (22)

Test 27

Name _____ Total Score _____

Date _____   Basic Score   100

Basic Time — 8 Minutes   Improvement Score _____

1. Compare these football teams as to average weights: (18 each average)

POSITION	TEAM 1 WEIGHT	TEAM 2 WEIGHT	TEAM 3 WEIGHT
C.	151	150	165
R. G.	175	171	170
L. G.	197	165	166
R. T.	217	171	182
L. T.	172	180	184
R. E.	171	174	153
L. E.	142	155	163
Q. B.	168	156	146
R. H.	160	153	168
L. H.	144	140	154
F. B.	155	180	162
Total			
Average			

2. Compare these years as to average monthly sales: (49 each average)

MONTH	LAST YEAR	THIS YEAR
January	$96,354	$98,847
February	125,721	135,768
March	106,349	116,853
April	113,762	123,918
May	95,926	94,025
June	103,451	112,736
July	84,673	89,529
August	132,426	148,285
September	115,392	121,728
October	94,236	105,845
November	97,512	112,756
December	136,457	143,568
Total		
Average		

3. Compare departments of a store as to average number of customers: (6 each average)

DAY	SHOES	JEWELRY	APPLIANCES
1st	326	314	318
2d	302	296	305
3d	333	340	321
4th	357	338	343
Total			
Average			

4. Compare daily attendance averages: (10 each average)

DAY	GRADE 1	GRADE 2	GRADE 3
Monday	926	945	913
Tuesday	948	956	928
Wednesday	1,012	1,059	989
Thursday	1,015	1,057	992
Friday	996	998	974
Total			
Average			

Exercise 28 — Application Problems

BASIC TIME — 10 Minutes *(Estimated time to obtain a basic score of 100)*

Solve these problems. Write the answers in the spaces on the right. (20 each)

1. If a worker saved $27 each week, how much would be saved in 48 weeks? .... _____

2. Nancy Kessler traveled 1,296 miles on a train. The train averaged 54 miles an hour. How many hours were needed for this train trip? .... _____

3. A total of 192 typewriter ribbons were used in a department containing 24 typewriters. On the average, how many ribbons were used on each machine? .... _____

4. How many articles are contained in 12 cases of merchandise if each case contains 12 cartons and each carton contains 2 dozen articles? .... _____

5. A sales representative reported the following mileage for last week: Monday, 21 miles; Tuesday, 109 miles; Wednesday, 95 miles; Thursday, 23 miles; Friday, 92 miles. What is the average mileage per day? .... _____

6. How many gallons of fuel will be used by a 4-engine airplane on a flight of 6 hours if each engine uses 46 gallons of fuel an hour? .... _____

7. The teacher has 12 boxes of pencils with 25 pencils in each box. If these pencils were divided evenly among 50 students, how many pencils would each person get? .... _____

8. A machine can print reports at an average rate of 576 an hour. How many reports can the machine print during a 5-day week if it is operated 3 hours a day? .... _____

9. John Leone bought a new car that was covered by a guarantee that remains effective for the first 24,000 miles the car is driven or for two years, whichever occurs first. During the first 12 months, he drove the car 18,000 miles. If he continues to average the same mileage each month, for how many more months can he expect his guarantee to remain in effect? .... _____

10. A typist transcribed 943 words in 41 minutes. How many words a minute did the typist average? .... _____

Test 28

Name _____ Total Score _____

Date _____ Basic Score ___100___

Basic Time — 8 Minutes Improvement Score _____

Solve these problems. Write the answers in the spaces on the right. (20 each)

1. A total of 884,304 nails was used in the construction of a building. If there were 69 nails to a pound, how many pounds of nails were required? .... _____

2. A typist had the following speed scores for a series of typewriting timings: 27, 28, 26, 31, 30, 32, 37, 33, and 35. What was the average score for this typist? .... _____

3. The combined weights of Gail and Audrey total 260 pounds. If Gail weighs 125 pounds, who weighs more — Gail or Audrey? By how much? .... _____

4. How many bags, each containing 4 dozen pears, can be filled from 10 cases of pears if each case holds 30 dozen? .... _____

5. Four heirs equally divided an estate of $520,000. Later a missing heir was located. How much must each of the original four heirs give to the fifth heir so that the estate will be equally divided among them? .... _____

6. A used car dealer has 5 cars priced at $3,250 each; 9 cars at $2,349 each; 10 cars at $11,990 each; 8 cars at $9,990 each; 7 cars at $7,890 each; and 6 cars at $5,690 each. What is the total value of these cars according to the prices listed? .. _____

7. On an automobile trip, the Jacob family had 1,209 miles to travel. The family drove 381 miles the first day but only 77 miles the second day because of a delay caused by engine trouble. The third day they drove 493 miles. How much farther did they have to drive? .... _____

8. Bruce earns $1,950 a month. Jason earns $390 a week. In one year (52 weeks), at these salaries, how much more will Bruce earn than Jason? .... _____

9. Elaine Strauss bought a new car 23 months ago. The automobile was covered by a guarantee that remains effective for the first 50,000 miles the car is driven or for five years, whichever occurs first. Elaine has now driven the car for 28,750 miles. For how many more months can she expect the guarantee to remain in effect? ...... _____

10. Sound travels at about 1,087 feet per second. In how many seconds will the report of an explosion be heard by someone who is 16,305 feet away from it? .... _____

Exercise 29: Signed Numbers — Addition and Multiplication

The rules for adding **signed numbers** are as follows. (1) To add numbers with like signs, add the numerical values and attach the common sign to the total. (2) To add two numbers with unlike signs, find the difference in the numerical values and attach the sign of the number with the larger numerical value to the total. A number that does not have a sign is assumed to be a positive number.

The rules for multiplying signed numbers are as follows. (1) To multiply two signed numbers, find the product of their numerical values. If the factors (each of the two numbers multiplied) have like signs, the product is positive. If the factors have unlike signs, the product is negative. (2) When multiplying more than two signed numbers, the product is positive if there is an even number of negative factors; the product is negative if there is an odd number of negative factors. Parentheses may be used instead of a times sign to show multiplication.

Example A
  − 8
  − 5
  − 6
  −19

Example B
  −43
  +22
  −21

Example C
  −5
   2
  −8
   9
  −2

Example D
$(-9)(-6) = +54$

Example E
$(-9)(6) = -54$

Example F
$(-6)(-4)(7)(-2) = -336$

BASIC TIME — 10 Minutes *(Estimated time to obtain a basic score of 100)*

Add these signed numbers: (6 each)

1. +12, −5
2. +8, +6
3. −9, −7
4. +12, −25
5. −9, +23
6. −15, −32
7. +18, −46, +20
8. −16, 45, −31

9. −85, 32, 27
10. −14, −23, −15
11. +26, +14, −39, −15
12. −8, 12, −20, 18
13. −15, −23, 1, 21
14. −16, −33, 75, −26
15. −9, 17, 26, −35, 57
16. 56, −62, −44, 31

Multiply these signed numbers: (8 each)

17. +16, +4
18. −34, −9
19. −52, 6
20. 79, −8
21. 68, 7

22. −45, −5
23. 12, −8
24. −37, 6
25. −64, −7
26. −92, −9

27. $(-2)(+5)(-3)(-4) =$ _____
28. $(+4)(-3)(5)(-6)(+2) =$ _____

29. $(-3)(+2)(-4)(-3)(+5)(-2)(3)(-4) =$ _____

Test 29

Name _____ Total Score _____
Date _____ Basic Score   100
Basic Time — 9 Minutes   Improvement Score _____

Add these signed numbers: (6 each)

1. +24
     7

2. −19
    −8

3. +46
    −9

4. −36
    +37

5. −8
    −17

6. −27
    +44

7. −26
     58
    −32

8.   28
    −57
     43

9.   97
     44
    −39

10. −26
    −54
     28

11. 38
    −26
     47
    −34

12. −7
    24
    32
    −40

13. 24
    −32
    −10
    +1

14. 25
    −42
     66
    −17

15. −12
    −9
     17
    −24
     48

16. −47
     53
    −1
     35
    −22

Multiply these signed numbers: (8 each)

17. +25
    +5

18. −47
    −3

19. 59
    −6

20. −18
     9

21. 36
    −12

22. 82
     4

23. −46
    −5

24. −93
    −7

25. 63
    −9

26. −81
     8

27. (−5)(−3)(4)(−6) = _____

28. (−4)(6)(−3)(−5)(−2) = _____

29. (+3)(−2)(5)(−2)(2)(−4)(5)(−3)(−2) = _____

Exercise 30: Signed Numbers — Division and Subtraction

To divide signed numbers, find the quotient of their numerical values. If the numbers have like signs, the quotient is positive. If the numbers have unlike signs, the quotient is negative. Note that $\frac{10}{5}$ means the same as $5\overline{)10}$ or $10 \div 5$.

To subtract signed numbers, change the sign of the subtrahend and add. "Subtract +9 from +17" (Example E below) becomes "Add the signed numbers 17 and −9."

Example A

$\frac{10}{5} = 2$

Check: $5 \times 2 = 10$

Example B

$\frac{10}{-5} = -2$

Check: $-5 \times -2 = 10$

Example C

$\frac{-10}{5} = -2$

Check: $5 \times -2 = -10$

Example D

$\frac{-10}{-5} = 2$

Check: $-5 \times 2 = -10$

Example E

Subtract: +17
         + 9

Solution: +17
         − 9

Answer: + 8

Example F

Subtract: −17
         − 9

Solution: −17
         + 9

Answer: − 8

Example G

Subtract: +17
         − 9

Solution: +17
         + 9

Answer: +26

Example H

Subtract: −17
         + 9

Solution: −17
         − 9

Answer: −26

BASIC TIME — 10 Minutes *(Estimated time to obtain a basic score of 100)*

Divide these signed numbers: (6 each)

1. $\frac{+35}{+7} =$ _____
2. $\frac{30}{-6} =$ _____
3. $\frac{-48}{+8} =$ _____
4. $\frac{-54}{-9} =$ _____

5. $\frac{-88}{8} =$ _____
6. $\frac{-75}{-5} =$ _____
7. $\frac{108}{-9} =$ _____
8. $\frac{-84}{7} =$ _____

9. $\frac{96}{-4} =$ _____
10. $\frac{112}{7} =$ _____
11. $\frac{-96}{-8} =$ _____
12. $\frac{-108}{6} =$ _____

13. $\frac{144}{8} =$ _____
14. $\frac{-56}{7} =$ _____
15. $\frac{45}{-5} =$ _____
16. $\frac{-6}{-1} =$ _____

Subtract these signed numbers: (8 each)

17. +16
    + 9

18. +15
    − 8

19. −18
    +14

20. −28
    − 17

21. 27
   −51

22. −38
    46

23. −48
    −54

24. 64
   52

25. 6
  −4

26. −37
    37

27. 64
   76

28. −72
   −85

29. 250
  −183

Test 30

Name _____ Total Score _____
Date _____ Basic Score 100
Basic Time — 9 Minutes Improvement Score _____

Divide these signed numbers: (6 each)

1. $\dfrac{+56}{+8} =$ _____
2. $\dfrac{84}{-6} =$ _____
3. $\dfrac{-98}{-7} =$ _____
4. $\dfrac{-72}{+9} =$ _____

5. $\dfrac{68}{-4} =$ _____
6. $\dfrac{-96}{-12} =$ _____
7. $\dfrac{-112}{8} =$ _____
8. $\dfrac{205}{-5} =$ _____

9. $\dfrac{-92}{4} =$ _____
10. $\dfrac{126}{7} =$ _____
11. $\dfrac{135}{-5} =$ _____
12. $\dfrac{-162}{-6} =$ _____

13. $\dfrac{-119}{-7} =$ _____
14. $\dfrac{108}{-9} =$ _____
15. $\dfrac{-32}{-8} =$ _____
16. $\dfrac{-15}{1} =$ _____

Subtract these signed numbers: (8 each)

17. +17
    +28
    ‾

18. -12
    - 4
    ‾

19.   28
    -40
    ‾

20. -36
     65
    ‾

21. -35
     32
    ‾

22.   87
    -97
    ‾

23.   23
     58
    ‾

24. -76
    -48
    ‾

25. -30
     17
    ‾

26.   20
    -19
    ‾

27. -52
    -74
    ‾

28. -18
     18
    ‾

29. -145
     -78
    ‾

Exercise 31 Solving Equations

Solving an equation unravels a mystery — the mystery of the value of *x* or some other symbol that is used to represent a number in an equation. In solving an equation, the terms are rearranged so that the term representing the unknown quantity appears on one side of the equals sign and the numerals appear on the other side.

A popular method of solving equations is based on **transposition**. To *transpose* means to transfer a term from one side of the equals sign to the other. This method is based on the following principle:

When an addend or subtrahend is transferred from one side of the equals sign to the other, its sign is changed from positive to negative or from negative to positive.

The answer obtained in solving an equation should be checked by substituting that value in the equation in place of the symbol for the unknown quantity. If the answer is correct, the left side of the equation will truly equal the right side.

Example A
Find the value of x in the equation $x + 7 = 23$.

Solution
$x + 7 = 23$
$x = 23 - 7$
$x = 16$

Check
$16 + 7 = 23$
$23 = 23$

Example B
Solve the equation $N - 8 = 32$.

Solution
$N - 8 = 32$
$N = 32 + 8$
$N = 40$

Check
$40 - 8 = 32$
$32 = 32$

BASIC TIME — 10 Minutes *(Estimated time to obtain a basic score of 100)*

Solve these equations. After checking each answer, place it in the appropriate space on the right. (20 each)

1. $x + 23 = 51$
2. $n + 18 = 35$
3. $43 + y = 87$
4. $58 + z = 72$
5. $n - 36 = 64$
6. $x - 39 = 25$
7. $y + 78 = 37$
8. $56 + z = 30$
9. $42 = n - 24$
10. $83 = x + 56$

1. _____
2. _____
3. _____
4. _____
5. _____
6. _____
7. _____
8. _____
9. _____
10. _____

64

Test 31

Name	Total Score	
Date	Basic Score	100
Basic Time — 10 Minutes	Improvement Score	

Solve these equations. Check each answer and place it in the appropriate space on the right. (20 each)

1. $n + 16 = 78$ 2. $x - 33 = 43$ 1. _____

2. _____

3. $y - 7 = 64$ 4. $z + 72 = 42$ 3. _____

4. _____

5. $18 + n = 72$ 6. $24 = x - 47$ 5. _____

6. _____

7. $y + 54 = 35$ 8. $44 + z = 59$ 7. _____

8. _____

9. $79 = x + 28$ 10. $55 = n - 39$ 9. _____

10. _____

Exercise 32: Multiplying and Collecting Terms in Equations

One method of showing multiplication is to closely join the symbols. That is, $5n$ means 5 *times* n, and $4(x + 1)$ means 4 *times* the quantity of $x + 1$.

When a multiplier or divisor is transferred from one side of an equals sign to the other side, its sign is changed from x to ÷ or from ÷ to x.

Notice in Examples A and B that the symbol being transferred is placed to the right of the symbols already on that side of the equals sign.

Example A

Solve this equation: $z \div 5 = 34$

Solution: $z \div 5 = 34$
$z = 34 \times 5$
$z = 170$

Check: $170 \div 5 = 34$
$34 = 34$

Example B

Solve this equation: $10n - 42 = 4n + 48$

Solution: $10n - 42 = 4n + 48$
$10n - 4n = 48 + 42$
$6n = 90$
$n = 90 \div 6$
$n = 15$

Check: $(10 \times 15) - 42 = (4 \times 15) + 48$
$150 - 42 = 60 + 48$
$108 = 108$

BASIC TIME — 18 Minutes *(Estimated time to obtain a basic score of 100)*

Solve these equations. Check each answer and place it in the appropriate space on the right. (20 each)

1. $9n = 369$
2. $15x = 780$
3. $y \div 7 = 84$
4. $z \div 9 = 72$
5. $3x + 6 = 18$
6. $3x - 7 = 38$
7. $5y - 75 = 3y + 17$
8. $86 - 7z = z + 46$
9. $3x + x + 2x = 105 - x$
10. $3n - 2 = 5n - 3n + 40$

1. _____
2. _____
3. _____
4. _____
5. _____
6. _____
7. _____
8. _____
9. _____
10. _____

Test 32

Name _____ Total Score _____
Date _____ Basic Score   100
Basic Time — 17 Minutes   Improvement Score _____

Solve these equations. Check each answer and place it in the appropriate space on the right. (20 each)

1. $22x = 748$

2. $41n = 1{,}722$

1. _____

2. _____

3. $y \div 65 = 9$

4. $8z + 16 = 760$

3. _____

4. _____

5. $7n - 27 = 421$

6. $58 + 4x = 414$

5. _____

6. _____

7. $8n + 94 = 3n + 124$

8. $10x - 23 = 6x + 77$

7. _____

8. _____

9. $3 + 5y + 6 + y = 159 - 4y$

10. $9z + 15 = 7z - 25 + 4z$

9. _____

10. _____

Exercise 33 — Order of Operations

The order in which the arithmetic operations should be done when solving an equation are as follows. (1) Do all operations that are in parentheses or in other signs of aggregation, such as brackets or braces. (2) Do all multiplications and divisions as they occur from left to right. (3) Do all additions and subtractions as they occur from left to right.

In Example A the parentheses show that the 11 and 2 are grouped together, so the operation of addition is done first.

Example A
$x = 23 - (11 + 2)$
$x = 23 - 13$
$x = 10$

In Example B the product of the first three factors is to be divided by the product of 3×5, or divided by the 3 and the result divided by 5.

Example B
$n = 2 \times 7 \times 75 \div (3 \times 5)$
$n = 1,050 \div 15$ [or $1,050 \div 3 \div 5$]
$n = 70$

Example C illustrates all of the three rules for the order of operations.

Example C
$y = 26 - 8 \times 12 \div (6 - 2) + 9$
$y = 26 - 8 \times 12 \div 4 + 9$
$y = 26 - 96 \div 4 + 9$
$y = 26 - 24 + 9$
$y = 11$

1. Do operations within parentheses first and eliminate the parentheses.
2. Multiply and divide from left to right.
3. Add and subtract from left to right.

BASIC TIME — 20 Minutes *(Estimated time to obtain a basic score of 100)*

For each of the following, indicate which operation should be done first. Place each answer in the appropriate space. (10 each)

1. $(30 - 6) \times 3$ _____
2. $30 + 6 \div 3$ _____
3. $(30 + 6) \div 3$ _____
4. $32 - 2 \times 4$ _____
5. $25 + 7 \times 4$ _____

Solve each of the following equations. Place each answer in the appropriate space. (10 each)

6. $n = 324 \div 36 \times 3$ _____
7. $y = 18 \times 30 + 24 \times 12$ _____
8. $x = 720 \div (45 \times 2)$ _____
9. $a = 35 + 28 \times 21 - 14$ _____
10. $z = 32 \times 16 - 16 + 56$ _____
11. $a = 72 \times 40 - 48 \div 24$ _____
12. $b = 48 \times 36 + 72 \div 24$ _____
13. $c = 224 - (140 \div 35)$ _____
14. $x = 208 - (117 \div 13)$ _____
15. $y = (104 \times 130 - 26) \div 78$ _____
16. $n = (450 + 30 \times 75) \div 150$ _____
17. $x = (224 \times 140 - 112 \times 168) \div (240 - 44)$ _____
18. $z = (81 \times 54 + 261 \times 108) \div (135 + 108)$ _____
19. $y = (160 \div 40 + 32 \times 16) \div (3 \times 4)$ _____
20. $n = (392 \div 8 + 35 \times 14) \div (7 \times 7)$ _____

68

Test 33

Name _____ Total Score _____

Date _____ Basic Score __100__

Basic Time — 22 Minutes Improvement Score _____

Complete each of the following statements by supplying the missing word(s). Place each answer in the appropriate space on the right. (8 each)

1. Regarding the order of arithmetic operations, after all signs of aggregation are eliminated, the operations of __?__ and __?__ should be done .... _____

2. The final step in the rules for the order of arithmetic operations is to do all __?__ and __?__ as they occur from left to right .... _____

3. In (20 − 10) ÷ 2, the first arithmetic operation to perform is __?__ .... _____

4. To find the value of x in $x = 5 − (10 + 3)$, the first arithmetic operation to perform is __?__ .... _____

5. To solve the equation $n = 40 − 9 + 3$, the arithmetic operation you should do first is __?__ .... _____

6. In $z = 20 − 8 ÷ 4$, the arithmetic operation to do first is __?__ .... _____

7. In $32 + 2 \times 4$, the arithmetic operation to do first is __?__ .... _____

8. To solve the problem $n = 20 + 12 ÷ 4$, the arithmetic operation that should be done first is __?__ .... _____

9. In the problem $y = 14 − (5 + 3)$, the arithmetic operation that should be done first is __?__ .... _____

10. In the problem $y = 30 + 5 \times 2$, the arithmetic operation that should be done first is __?__ .... _____

Solve each of the following equations. (8 each)

11. $a = 54 + 31 \times 16 − 12$ .... _____
12. $n = 18 \times 30 + 24 ÷ 12$ .... _____
13. $y = 17 \times 20 + 35 \times 14$ .... _____
14. $b = 51 \times 40 − 72 ÷ 24$ .... _____
15. $x = (22 \times 14 − 12 \times 16) ÷ 58$ .... _____
16. $y = (81 \times 53) − (46 \times 39)$ .... _____
17. $z = (192 \times 96) ÷ (64 \times 32)$ .... _____
18. $c = 146 − (280 ÷ 14)$ .... _____
19. $x = 324 ÷ (36 \times 3)$ .... _____
20. $a = 36 + 12 \times 24 − 30$ .... _____
21. $n = (140 \times 32 − 16) ÷ 279$ .... _____
22. $x = (160 ÷ 40 + 32 \times 16) ÷ (27 + 16)$ .... _____
23. $y = (480 − 30 + 20 \times 55) ÷ (46 − 23 + 27)$ .... _____
24. $x = (46 \times 82) + (93 \times 58)$ .... _____
25. $n = (126 \times 84) ÷ (21 \times 14)$ .... _____

Exercise 34 — Parentheses in Equations

Parentheses are necessary in some equations to show which symbols are to be treated as one quantity. For example, $24 \div 2 + 4$ gives $12 + 4 = 16$; but, $24 \div (2 + 4)$ gives $24 \div 6 = 4$. The parentheses indicate that the 2 and 4 are associated (grouped together), so the addition should be done before the division. Parentheses and other signs of aggregation in an equation should be eliminated as soon as possible.

When parentheses that enclose addends and subtrahends are preceded by a factor, each symbol within the parentheses is multiplied by the factor. The example at the right shows the solution of the equation $5(n + 3) - 2(n - 4) = 173$.

Example

$5(n + 3) - 2(n - 4) = 173$
$5n + 15 - 2n + 8 = 173$
$5n - 2n = 173 - 15 - 8$
$3n = 150$
$n = 150 \div 3$
$n = 50$

Check

$5(50 + 3) - 2(50 - 4) = 173$
$5(53) - 2(46) = 173$
$265 - 92 = 173$
$173 = 173$

BASIC TIME — 24 Minutes *(Estimated time to obtain a basic score of 100)*

Solve these equations. Check each answer and place it in the appropriate space on the right. (10 each for Problems 1–6; 14 each for Problems 7–16)

1. $5(n + 6) = 45$
2. $3(x - 5) = x + 17$
3. $4(30 - 4y) = 4y + 500$
4. $16z = 4(20 - z)$
5. $16 - 2(a - 4) = a - 30$
6. $7b \div (6 - 4) = 63$
7. $14 + 3(x + 6) = 4 + 2(3x + 5)$
8. $10 + 5(y + 4) = 4(y + 3) + 8$
9. $160 - 4(n - 3) = 16$
10. $2(a - 4) + 3(a - 2) = 151$
11. $3(b + 2) - 4(b - 3) = 50$
12. $3(c - 3) - 2(c - 2) = 120$
13. $4(5n - 2) = 100 - 6(n + 5)$
14. $3(5x - 1) = 2(3x + 6) + 417$
15. $2(3y - 4) = 340 - 3(y - 4)$
16. $5(z + 3) - (4z - 8) = 130$

1. _____
2. _____
3. _____
4. _____
5. _____
6. _____
7. _____
8. _____
9. _____
10. _____
11. _____
12. _____
13. _____
14. _____
15. _____
16. _____

Test 34

Name _____ Total Score _____

Date _____ Basic Score ___100___

Basic Time — 22 Minutes Improvement Score _____

Solve these equations. Check each answer and place it in the appropriate space on the right. (20 each)

1. $7(n + 2) = 105$

2. $6(x - 4) = 5x + 20$

3. $60 - 5(y - 4) = y - 16$

4. $6 + 4(z + 2) = 2(z + 7) + 40$

5. $3(a + 4) - 6(a - 3) = 105$

6. $5(3b - 2) = 4(2b + 3) + 34$

7. $6(2c + 5) = 4(c - 20) - 2$

8. $5(5x + 20) = 3(x + 48)$

9. $5(y - 3) + 8 = 67 - (30 - y)$

10. $14z - 4(z + 2) = 2(z - 2) + 3(z - 8)$

1. _____

2. _____

3. _____

4. _____

5. _____

6. _____

7. _____

8. _____

9. _____

10. _____

Exercise 35 Algebraic Expressions

To change from words to algebraic terms, follow these two rules: (1) Select a symbol such as x to represent one of the unknown quantities. (2) Express each of the other unknown quantities in relation to that symbol.

Example A Candy costs n dollars a pound. Express each of the following:

Solutions:
- The cost of 5 pounds: $5n$
- The cost of x pounds: xn
- How much $3 will buy: $3 \div n$
- The cost of 4 pounds if price reduced $1 a pound: $4(n-1)$

Example B Mary is now x years old. Express her age for each of the following:

Solutions:
- Her age 3 years ago: $x - 3$
- Her age 5 years from now: $x + 5$
- Her age y years ago: $x - y$
- Her age n years from now: $x + n$
- Twice her present age: $2x$
- Half her present age: $x \div 2$

BASIC TIME — 25 Minutes *(Estimated time to obtain a basic score of 100)*

Use algebraic symbols to write each of the following. Place each answer in the appropriate space. (8 each)

1. a plus b ....
2. 4 more than x ....
3. x minus y ....
4. 3 less than z ....
5. r times b ....
6. p divided by r ....
7. One third of n ....
8. x decreased by 4 ....
9. 6 times the sum of a and b ....
10. y increased by one half of itself ....

Let x represent the length in feet of a certain board. Write an algebraic expression that represents the length of a board that is: (3 each)

11. 2 feet longer ....
12. 3 feet shorter ....
13. Twice as long ....
14. Half as long ....

If y represents Ruth's present age in years, what algebraic expression represents her age: (3 each)

15. 8 years from now? ....
16. 6 years ago? ....
17. b years ago? ....
18. c years from now? ....

Solve these problems. Place each answer in the appropriate space on the right. (12 each)

19. The difference between two numbers is 23. If the smaller number is represented by s, what algebraic expression represents the other number? ....

20. The sum of two numbers is represented by x. If one of the numbers is 34, what algebraic expression represents the other number? ....

21. Show the cost of 3 pounds of candy at z dollars a pound. ....

22. Write an algebraic expression to show four times the quantity of y plus five. ....

23. Show an algebraic expression that represents three times the sum of x and two. ....

24. Write an algebraic expression to show the sum of 35 and two times the quantity of n minus six. ....

25. Write an algebraic expression that represents the difference between 48 and twice the sum of x and four. ....

26. The selling price of one pound of candy is $6. Show an algebraic expression to represent the change returned if a $20 bill is given to pay for n pounds. ....

Test 35

Name _____ Total Score _____
Date _____ Basic Score __100__
Basic Time — 22 Minutes Improvement Score _____

Use algebraic symbols to write each of the following. Place each answer in the appropriate space on the right. (10 each)

1. 7 added to x .... _____
2. 5 more than n .... _____
3. 6 less than y .... _____
4. 3 times z .... _____
5. n divided by 8 .... _____
6. p times r .... _____
7. One half of x .... _____
8. 1.5 times y .... _____
9. 5 times the sum of z and 4 .... _____
10. n decreased by one third of itself .... _____

11. A computer (Brand XYZ) sells for x dollars and another (Brand ABC) sells for $800 more. Express the selling price of the Brand ABC computer .... _____

12. Write an algebraic expression for the number of months in y years .... _____

13. There were 200 gallons of milk in a tank. How many gallons were in the tank after z gallons of milk were added to the tank? .... _____

14. The price of one dozen ballpoint pens is n dollars. Express the price of one pen ... _____

15. One pencil costs x cents. Express the cost of one dozen pencils .... _____

16. Ida Williams earns d dollars a month and her brother, Leroy, earns $200 a month more. Express Leroy's (a) monthly earnings and (b) annual earnings. ....
    (a) _____
    (b) _____

17. An employee earns $400 a week and spends an average of x dollars a day. How much can this employee save in 8 weeks? .... _____

18. Richard Doty invested $50,000 in two investments. If n represents the number of dollars placed in the first investment, what expression represents the other? .... _____

19. The percentage, P, is the rate, R, times the base, B. Express this statement as an equation .... _____

20. The selling price of one doughnut is x cents and of one breakfast roll is y cents. Express the total selling price of 6 doughnuts and 12 rolls .... _____

Exercise 36 — Application Problems

There is no magic formula that can be used to guarantee finding the correct answer to every word problem. Following the rules below, however, can help you to solve most word problems.

1. Read the problem all the way through.
2. Determine what the problem asks.
3. Let a symbol such as x represent one of the unknown quantities.
4. Express the other unknown quantities in terms of this symbol.
5. Write an equation expressing the relationship between the given and the unknown quantities.
6. Solve the equation to find the value of the unknown quantities.
7. Check the solution.

BASIC TIME — 30 Minutes *(Estimated time to obtain a basic score of 100)*

Use an equation in good form to solve each of the following problems. Check each answer and write it in the appropriate space on the right. (10 each)

1. The sum of two numbers is 87. The smaller number is 15 less than the larger number. What is the larger number? ....

2. The sum of three consecutive even numbers is 822. Find the numbers. ....

3. The sum of three numbers is 163. The second number is twice the first, and the third is 15 more than the first. Find the numbers. ....

4. The sum of three consecutive odd numbers is 129. Find the numbers ....

5. If twice a certain number is increased by 40, the result is the same as when four times the number is increased by 6. Find the number. ....

6. The second of two numbers is four less than three times the first. The sum of the numbers is 188. Find the numbers. ....

7. The partnership agreement of Fletcher, Graves, and Harrington provides that when earnings and losses are distributed, Harrington is to get twice as much as Fletcher and that Graves is to get twice as much as Harrington. Earnings for the past year totaled $199,500. How much should go to (a) Fletcher, (b) Graves, and (c) Harrington? ....
   (a) _____
   (b) _____
   (c) _____

8. Alice Pence paid $18,000 in state and federal income taxes for the past year. The federal tax was four times as large as the state tax. How much did she pay in (a) state income tax and (b) federal income tax? ....
   (a) _____
   (b) _____

9. Cole and Davis invested $78,000 in a business. Davis invested $5,000 more than Cole. How much was invested by (a) Cole and (b) Davis? ....
   (a) _____
   (b) _____

10. When 79 is subtracted from three times a certain number, the result is the same as when 18 is subtracted from twice the number. Find the number. ....

11. Partners Brown and Campbell cleared $15,000 in a certain business transaction. By agreement Brown received three times as much as Campbell. How much should be distributed by the accountant to (a) Campbell and (b) Brown? ....
    (a) _____
    (b) _____

12. Mary drove 843 miles in two days. On the first day she drove 75 miles farther than she did the second day. How far did she drive the first day? ....

13. Ruemmler and Simmons invested $67,500 in a business. Ruemmler invested $3,500 more than Simmons. How much did Simmons invest in the business? ....

14. Thirty bills of currency consisting of $5 bills and $10 bills totaled $235. Find the number of (a) $5 bills and (b) $10 bills. ....
    (a) _____
    (b) _____

Test 36

Name _____ Total Score _____
Date _____   Basic Score   100
Basic Time — 30 Minutes   Improvement Score _____

Use an equation in good form to solve each of the following problems. Check each answer and write it in the appropriate space on the right. (10 each)

1. A number increased by 23 is 85. What is the number? .... _____

2. A number decreased by 35 is 97. What is the number? .... _____

3. Forty more than six times a number is 232. Find the number. .... _____

4. Nine less than five times a number is 276. Find the number. .... _____

5. When 19 is subtracted from a number, the result is 89. What is the number? ...... _____

6. The sum of three numbers is 156. The second number is 4 more than the first, and the third is 14 more than the first. Find the numbers. .... _____

7. Ruth has $25 more than Susan. Together they have $247. How many dollars does Susan have? .... _____

8. Six times a certain number equals the number increased by 165. What is the number? .... _____

9. The sum of three consecutive odd numbers is 237. Find the numbers. .... _____

10. Lew is three years older than David. The sum of their ages is 49. How old are (a) David and (b) Lew? .... (a) _____ (b) _____

11. If four times a certain number is increased by 53, the result is the same as when seven times the number is decreased by 34. Find the number. .... _____

12. The second of two numbers is eight less than four times the first. The sum of the numbers is 267. Find the numbers. .... _____

13. The partnership agreement of Keplar, Lowery, and Mundell provides that when earnings and losses are distributed, Mundell is to get three times as much as Keplar and that Lowery is to get twice as much as Mundell. Earnings for the past year totaled $240,000. How much should go to (a) Keplar, (b) Lowery, and (c) Mundell? .... (a) _____ (b) _____ (c) _____

14. A house and lot together cost $167,500. The house cost $107,500 more than the lot. Find the cost of (a) the lot and (b) the house. .... _____

15. Allen and Baker invested $68,000 in a business. Baker invested $7,000 more than Allen. How much was invested by (a) Allen and (b) Baker? .... (a) _____ (b) _____

16. When 93 is added to five times a certain number, the result is the same as when 29 is added to seven times the number. Find the number. .... _____

17. When they entered into partnership, Edwards and Frailey agreed that Frailey would receive twice as much as Edwards when gains and losses were distributed. How much of a loss of $123,540 should go to (a) Edwards and (b) Frailey? ... (a) _____ (b) _____

18. A coat and dress together cost $185. The coat cost $57 more than the dress. How much did the dress cost? .... _____

19. Neal and Odum invested $67,500 in a business. Neal invested $5,700 more than Odum. How much did Odum invest in the business? .... _____

20. Seventy-one bills of currency consisting of $5 bills and $10 bills totaled $530. Find the number of (a) $5 bills and (b) $10 bills .... (a) _____ (b) _____

Exercise 37 Common Denominator

A part of a whole number is called a **fraction**. A fraction expresses a relationship between two numbers. The top number of a fraction is the **numerator**. The bottom number is the **denominator**.

In addition and subtraction, only like denominations should be added or subtracted. In the addition of fractions, if the denominators are different, the fractions must be changed to equivalent fractions with a *common denominator*; that is, all denominators must be the same.

To change a fraction to its equivalent in a higher denomination, multiply the denominator by the number that will give the desired denominator; then multiply the numerator by the same number. See Example A.

Example A $\quad \frac{4}{5} = \frac{4 \times 4}{5 \times 4} = \frac{16}{20}$

To change a fraction to its equivalent in a lower denomination, divide both the numerator and denominator by the same number. See Example B.

Example B $\quad \frac{3}{12} = \frac{3 \div 3}{12 \div 3} = \frac{1}{4}$

BASIC TIME — 2 Minutes *(Estimated time to obtain a basic score of 100)*

	a	b	c	d	
Change to 12ths: 1.	$\frac{1}{2} = \frac{}{12}$	$\frac{2}{3} = \frac{}{12}$	$\frac{3}{4} = \frac{}{12}$	$\frac{5}{6} = \frac{}{12}$	(6)
Change to 32ds: 2.	$\frac{3}{4} = \frac{}{32}$	$\frac{5}{8} = \frac{}{32}$	$\frac{7}{8} = \frac{}{32}$	$\frac{9}{16} = \frac{}{32}$	(6)
Change to 72ds: 3.	$\frac{2}{3} = \frac{}{72}$	$\frac{3}{4} = \frac{}{72}$	$\frac{5}{6} = \frac{}{72}$	$\frac{7}{8} = \frac{}{72}$	(12)
Change to 4ths: 4.	$\frac{12}{16} = \frac{}{4}$	$\frac{18}{24} = \frac{}{4}$	$\frac{24}{32} = \frac{}{4}$	$\frac{42}{56} = \frac{}{4}$	(8)
Change to 9ths: 5.	$\frac{15}{27} = \frac{}{9}$	$\frac{45}{81} = \frac{}{9}$	$\frac{20}{36} = \frac{}{9}$	$\frac{42}{54} = \frac{}{9}$	(8)
Change to 16ths: 6.	$\frac{15}{48} = \frac{}{16}$	$\frac{25}{80} = \frac{}{16}$	$\frac{28}{64} = \frac{}{16}$	$\frac{18}{32} = \frac{}{16}$	(10)

Test 37

Change to higher or lower terms as indicated:

	a	b	c	d	
1.	$\frac{1}{2} = \frac{}{8}$	$\frac{1}{3} = \frac{}{12}$	$\frac{1}{4} = \frac{}{32}$	$\frac{1}{6} = \frac{}{72}$	(4)
2.	$\frac{2}{3} = \frac{}{48}$	$\frac{3}{4} = \frac{}{32}$	$\frac{5}{6} = \frac{}{24}$	$\frac{7}{8} = \frac{}{64}$	(6)
3.	$\frac{11}{12} = \frac{}{72}$	$\frac{13}{16} = \frac{}{64}$	$\frac{19}{24} = \frac{}{72}$	$\frac{17}{32} = \frac{}{96}$	(8)
4.	$\frac{3}{16} = \frac{}{48}$	$\frac{5}{9} = \frac{}{63}$	$\frac{7}{13} = \frac{}{52}$	$\frac{9}{17} = \frac{}{68}$	(7)
5.	$\frac{4}{16} = \frac{}{4}$	$\frac{6}{8} = \frac{}{4}$	$\frac{12}{16} = \frac{}{4}$	$\frac{12}{15} = \frac{}{5}$	(4)
6.	$\frac{20}{25} = \frac{}{5}$	$\frac{20}{24} = \frac{}{6}$	$\frac{24}{36} = \frac{}{3}$	$\frac{18}{30} = \frac{}{5}$	(6)
7.	$\frac{20}{32} = \frac{}{8}$	$\frac{14}{21} = \frac{}{3}$	$\frac{15}{27} = \frac{}{9}$	$\frac{21}{24} = \frac{}{8}$	(4)
8.	$\frac{30}{36} = \frac{}{6}$	$\frac{16}{36} = \frac{}{9}$	$\frac{21}{56} = \frac{}{8}$	$\frac{20}{45} = \frac{}{9}$	(4)
9.	$\frac{7}{8} = \frac{}{72}$	$\frac{5}{25} = \frac{}{5}$	$\frac{9}{16} = \frac{}{80}$	$\frac{13}{52} = \frac{}{4}$	(7)

Exercise 38 — Lowest Terms of Common Fractions

Numbers such as $\frac{1}{2}$, $\frac{3}{4}$, and $\frac{10}{12}$, in which the numerators are smaller than the denominators, are called **common fractions**. It is necessary to know how to reduce common fractions to lowest terms when they are not already so expressed. To change a common fraction to its lowest terms, divide the numerator and the denominator by all the divisors that are common to both. See Example A.

Example A $\quad \frac{18}{24} = \frac{18 \div 2}{24 \div 2} = \frac{9}{12} ; \frac{9}{12} = \frac{9 \div 3}{12 \div 3} = \frac{3}{4}$

When a common divisor cannot be seen readily, find the **greatest common divisor (gcd)**. See Example B.

Example B Change $\frac{39}{65}$ to its lowest terms.

Solution: $\frac{39 \div 13}{65 \div 13} = \frac{3}{5}$

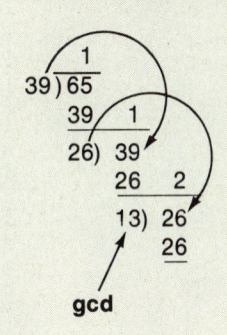

```
        1
    39)65
       39      1
       26)39
          26    2
          13)26
             26
 gcd
```

Divide the larger number by the smaller. Then divide the remainder into the preceding divisor. Continue this procedure until there is no remainder. The *last divisor* is the greatest common divisor (gcd).

BASIC TIME —4 Minutes *(Estimated time to obtain a basic score of 100)*

Find the *gcd* and change each fraction to lowest terms: (198 points)

	a	b	c	
1.	$\frac{12}{16} =$ gcd____	$\frac{24}{64} =$ gcd____	$\frac{18}{32} =$ gcd____	(8) (2)
2.	$\frac{9}{24} =$ gcd____	$\frac{18}{30} =$ gcd____	$\frac{15}{72} =$ gcd____	(8) (2)
3.	$\frac{24}{84} =$ gcd____	$\frac{15}{60} =$ gcd____	$\frac{28}{96} =$ gcd____	(12) (2)
4.	$\frac{57}{95} =$ gcd____	$\frac{91}{156} =$ gcd____	$\frac{51}{85} =$ gcd____	(14) (2)
5.	$\frac{46}{115} =$ gcd____	$\frac{58}{87} =$ gcd____	$\frac{63}{155} =$ gcd____	(14) (2)

Test 38

78

Name _____ Total Score _____
Date _____ Basic Score __100__
Basic Time — 3 Minutes Improvement Score _____

Change to lowest terms: (198 points)

            a   b   c

1. $\dfrac{15}{36} =$ $\dfrac{36}{66} =$ $\dfrac{18}{54} =$ (10)

2. $\dfrac{48}{72} =$ $\dfrac{24}{40} =$ $\dfrac{63}{81} =$ (10)

3. $\dfrac{28}{98} =$ $\dfrac{90}{145} =$ $\dfrac{56}{104} =$ (14)

4. $\dfrac{32}{144} =$ $\dfrac{48}{116} =$ $\dfrac{27}{108} =$ (16)

5. $\dfrac{39}{91} =$ $\dfrac{24}{84} =$ $\dfrac{48}{92} =$ (16)

Exercise 39 — Improper Fractions and Mixed Numbers

Numbers such as $2\frac{1}{2}$, $5\frac{3}{4}$, and $6\frac{2}{5}$, which are composed of a whole number and a fraction, are **mixed numbers**. Fractions such as $\frac{4}{4}$, $\frac{7}{5}$, and $\frac{8}{3}$, in which the numerator is as large as or larger than the denominator, are **improper fractions**.

Every mixed number can be expressed as an improper fraction. To change a mixed number to an improper fraction, multiply the whole number by the denominator and to this product add the numerator. This final number will be the numerator of the improper fraction. The denominator will not change. See Example A.

To change an improper fraction to a mixed number, divide the numerator by the denominator. The quotient will be the whole number. The remainder (if there is one) will be placed over the denominator of the original improper fraction to form the fractional part of the mixed number. See Example B.

Example A

$$4\frac{3}{5} = \frac{(4 \times 5) + 3}{5} = \frac{23}{5}$$

Example B

$$\frac{23}{5} = 5\overline{)23} = 4\frac{3}{5}$$
$$\phantom{\frac{23}{5} = }\underline{20}$$
$$\phantom{\frac{23}{5} = 5\overline{)}}3$$

BASIC TIME — 3 Minutes *(Estimated time to obtain a basic score of 100)*

Change to improper fractions: (198 points)

	a	b	c	
1.	$2\frac{3}{4} =$	$5\frac{5}{8} =$	$6\frac{7}{8} =$	(3)
2.	$9\frac{11}{12} =$	$12\frac{7}{12} =$	$8\frac{9}{16} =$	(5)
3.	$15\frac{17}{32} =$	$21\frac{15}{16} =$	$25\frac{7}{15} =$	(12)
4.	$3\frac{19}{64} =$	$5\frac{17}{48} =$	$23\frac{11}{27} =$	(12)

Change to mixed numbers:

5.	$\frac{17}{5} =$	$\frac{35}{8} =$	$\frac{47}{32} =$	(4)
6.	$\frac{53}{6} =$	$\frac{55}{12} =$	$\frac{49}{9} =$	(4)
7.	$\frac{121}{64} =$	$\frac{144}{17} =$	$\frac{156}{23} =$	(12)
8.	$\frac{541}{16} =$	$\frac{642}{9} =$	$\frac{463}{24} =$	(14)

Test 39

Name _____ Total Score _____
Date _____ Basic Score ___100___
Basic Time — 3 Minutes Improvement Score _____

Change to improper fractions: (198 points)

	a	b	c	
1.	$7\frac{1}{4} =$	$6\frac{3}{8} =$	$4\frac{4}{9} =$	(3)
2.	$8\frac{5}{12} =$	$9\frac{8}{11} =$	$7\frac{3}{16} =$	(4)
3.	$13\frac{11}{16} =$	$12\frac{5}{32} =$	$15\frac{13}{15} =$	(14)
4.	$5\frac{19}{64} =$	$6\frac{17}{48} =$	$13\frac{5}{17} =$	(14)

Change to mixed numbers:

	a	b	c	
5.	$\frac{18}{5} =$	$\frac{27}{8} =$	$\frac{35}{12} =$	(4)
6.	$\frac{62}{7} =$	$\frac{53}{16} =$	$\frac{72}{15} =$	(5)
7.	$\frac{73}{32} =$	$\frac{137}{64} =$	$\frac{169}{48} =$	(8)
8.	$\frac{657}{19} =$	$\frac{329}{24} =$	$\frac{427}{63} =$	(14)

Exercise 40 — Lowest Common Denominator

A number that is divisible, without a remainder, by a set of numbers is a **common multiple** of that set. A number larger than 1 that is divisible only by 1 and by itself is a **prime number**. For example, 2, 3, 5, 7, 11, and 13 are the six smallest prime numbers.

A set of numbers will have many common multipliers. The smallest of these is the **lowest common multiple (lcm)**. To find the *lcm* of a set of numbers, arrange the numbers in a horizontal row and divide by any prime number common to two or more of the numbers of the set. Carry down each quotient together with any number that is not divisible by the chosen prime number. Continue dividing in this manner until no two numbers can be divided by a prime number. Then multiply together all the prime number divisors and the final quotients.

The lowest common multiple of the denominators in a set of fractions is the **lowest common denominator (lcd)**.

Example Find the lowest common multiple *(lcm)* of 8, 16, 20, and 25.

Solution:

```
2)8   16   20   25
2)4    8   10   25
2)2    4    5   25
5)1    2    5   25
   1    2    1    5   ← final quotients
```

$2 \times 2 \times 2 \times 5 \times 1 \times 2 \times 1 \times 5 = 400$ **lcm**

400 is the smallest number into which 8, 16, 20, and 25 will divide.

BASIC TIME — 8 Minutes *(Estimated time to obtain a basic score of 100)*

Find the lowest common multiple of each set of numbers. Place each answer in the appropriate space on the right.

1. 8, 12, 15, 20
2. 16, 20, 24, 40
3. 25, 35, 42, 45
4. 16, 18, 25, 35
5. 24, 32, 35, 50
6. 32, 42, 48, 52

1. _____ (20)
2. _____ (20)
3. _____ (20)
4. _____ (20)
5. _____ (24)
6. _____ (24)

Find the lowest common denominator of each set of fractions. Place each answer in the appropriate space on the right.

7. $\dfrac{5}{6}, \dfrac{7}{8}, \dfrac{5}{9}, \dfrac{7}{12}$
8. $\dfrac{8}{15}, \dfrac{9}{16}, \dfrac{13}{20}, \dfrac{11}{32}$
9. $\dfrac{9}{16}, \dfrac{7}{12}, \dfrac{5}{8}, \dfrac{11}{32}$
10. $\dfrac{5}{12}, \dfrac{15}{32}, \dfrac{11}{48}, \dfrac{19}{64}$

7. _____ (16)
8. _____ (16)
9. _____ (20)
10. _____ (20)

Test 40

Name _____ Total Score _____
Date _____ Basic Score   100
Basic Time — 7 Minutes   Improvement Score _____

Find the lowest common multiple of each set of numbers. Place each answer in the appropriate space on the right.

1. 6, 8, 9, 12, 15
2. 15, 16, 18, 20, 24

1. _____(20)

2. _____(20)

3. 7, 8, 9, 10, 16
4. 20, 25, 30, 35, 40

3. _____(20)

4. _____(20)

Find the lowest common denominator of each set of fractions. Place each answer in the appropriate space on the right.

5. $\frac{7}{8}, \frac{5}{12}, \frac{3}{16}, \frac{17}{24}$
6. $\frac{14}{15}, \frac{11}{20}, \frac{17}{25}, \frac{1}{30}$

5. _____(16)

6. _____(16)

7. $\frac{13}{18}, \frac{15}{32}, \frac{17}{48}, \frac{7}{64}$
8. $\frac{5}{9}, \frac{15}{16}, \frac{11}{24}, \frac{17}{30}$

7. _____(24)

8. _____(24)

9. $\frac{5}{18}, \frac{7}{24}, \frac{11}{32}, \frac{19}{40}$
10. $\frac{11}{16}, \frac{17}{20}, \frac{5}{28}, \frac{15}{32}$

9. _____(20)

10. _____(20)

Exercise 41 — Addition of Common Fractions

In order to add common fractions, all denominators must be the same. Therefore, change them to equivalent fractions with their lowest common denominator. Add the new numerators, and place this sum over the lowest common denominator. If the result is an improper fraction, change it to a mixed number in lowest terms.

When the lowest common denominator cannot be found through inspection, you can find it by following the procedure described in Exercise 40. In the example below, $\frac{2}{3}$ is added to $\frac{3}{4}$ by changing the two fractions to equivalent fractions with the lowest common denominator of 12.

Add: $\quad \frac{2}{3} + \frac{3}{4} = \frac{8}{12} + \frac{9}{12} = \frac{17}{12} = 1\frac{5}{12}$

BASIC TIME — 8 Minutes *(Estimated time to obtain a basic score of 100)*

Change to equivalent fractions with common denominators and add:

1. $\frac{1}{4} + \frac{2}{3} =$
2. $\frac{3}{4} + \frac{5}{6} =$
3. $\frac{4}{5} + \frac{3}{4} =$
4. $\frac{5}{8} + \frac{5}{6} =$
5. $\frac{5}{6} + \frac{4}{9} =$
6. $\frac{3}{5} + \frac{2}{3} =$
7. $\frac{5}{9} + \frac{4}{7} =$
8. $\frac{2}{5} + \frac{4}{9} =$
9. $\frac{15}{16} + \frac{5}{6} =$
10. $\frac{7}{12} + \frac{5}{8} =$
11. $\frac{15}{32} + \frac{7}{24} =$
12. $\frac{5}{9} + \frac{7}{16} =$
13. $\frac{1}{2} + \frac{2}{3} + \frac{3}{4} =$
14. $\frac{2}{3} + \frac{5}{8} + \frac{7}{12} =$
15. $\frac{7}{12} + \frac{5}{8} + \frac{5}{6} + \frac{2}{3} =$
16. $\frac{15}{32} + \frac{3}{8} + \frac{7}{16} + \frac{7}{24} =$

1. _____(10)
2. _____(10)
3. _____(10)
4. _____(10)
5. _____(10)
6. _____(10)
7. _____(12)
8. _____(12)
9. _____(13)
10. _____(13)
11. _____(13)
12. _____(13)
13. _____(15)
14. _____(15)
15. _____(17)
16. _____(17)

Test 41

Name _____ Total Score _____

Date _____ Basic Score __100__

Basic Time — 7 Minutes Improvement Score _____

Change to equivalent fractions with common denominators and add. Place each answer in the appropriate space on the right.

1. $\dfrac{3}{4} + \dfrac{1}{6} =$ 2. $\dfrac{3}{8} + \dfrac{5}{6} =$

3. $\dfrac{8}{9} + \dfrac{5}{8} =$ 4. $\dfrac{3}{5} + \dfrac{4}{9} =$

5. $\dfrac{5}{6} + \dfrac{7}{8} =$ 6. $\dfrac{3}{8} + \dfrac{7}{12} =$

7. $\dfrac{9}{16} + \dfrac{5}{9} =$ 8. $\dfrac{8}{25} + \dfrac{1}{2} =$

9. $\dfrac{5}{12} + \dfrac{7}{16} =$ 10. $\dfrac{7}{24} + \dfrac{5}{9} =$

11. $\dfrac{1}{4} + \dfrac{3}{8} + \dfrac{5}{6} =$ 12. $\dfrac{3}{5} + \dfrac{2}{3} + \dfrac{5}{8} =$

13. $\dfrac{2}{3} + \dfrac{1}{2} + \dfrac{4}{5} =$ 14. $\dfrac{7}{8} + \dfrac{2}{3} + \dfrac{1}{6} =$

15. $\dfrac{3}{4} + \dfrac{5}{8} + \dfrac{7}{16} + \dfrac{5}{12} =$ 16. $\dfrac{5}{16} + \dfrac{3}{5} + \dfrac{2}{3} + \dfrac{5}{8} =$

1. _____(10)
2. _____(10)
3. _____(10)
4. _____(10)
5. _____(10)
6. _____(10)
7. _____(11)
8. _____(11)
9. _____(12)
10. _____(12)
11. _____(15)
12. _____(15)
13. _____(15)
14. _____(15)
15. _____(17)
16. _____(17)

Exercise 42 — Addition of Mixed Numbers

To add mixed numbers, (1) add the whole numbers, (2) add the fractions, and (3) reduce the answer to lowest terms.

See the example at the right for the addition of $4\frac{2}{3} + 6\frac{3}{4}$.

Add: $4\frac{2}{3}$
$6\frac{3}{4}$

Solution: $4\frac{2}{3} = 4\frac{8}{12}$
$6\frac{3}{4} = 6\frac{9}{12}$
$\overline{\phantom{6\frac{3}{4} = }10\frac{17}{12} = 11\frac{5}{12}}$

BASIC TIME — 10 Minutes *(Estimated time to obtain a basic score of 100)*

Add the whole-number portions and the fractional parts of each problem separately and then combine the results. Place each answer in the appropriate space on the right.

1. $3\frac{7}{8}$
 $11\frac{13}{16}$

2. $2\frac{3}{4}$
 $5\frac{7}{12}$

3. $9\frac{1}{2}$
 $5\frac{1}{3}$

4. $4\frac{3}{8}$
 $14\frac{1}{6}$

1. _____ (12)
2. _____ (12)
3. _____ (12)
4. _____ (12)

5. $7\frac{1}{8}$
 $5\frac{1}{3}$

6. $2\frac{2}{3}$
 $3\frac{3}{5}$

7. $14\frac{5}{6}$
 $8\frac{2}{9}$

8. $10\frac{4}{9}$
 $14\frac{5}{7}$

5. _____ (14)
6. _____ (14)
7. _____ (14)
8. _____ (14)

9. $15\frac{7}{8}$
 $8\frac{5}{12}$

10. $6\frac{11}{16}$
 $12\frac{13}{24}$

11. $10\frac{5}{16}$
 $5\frac{7}{12}$

9. _____ (15)
10. _____ (15)
11. _____ (15)

12. $7\frac{3}{8}$
 $4\frac{1}{3}$
 $3\frac{4}{5}$

13. $3\frac{1}{2}$
 $4\frac{1}{3}$
 $5\frac{1}{5}$

14. $6\frac{2}{3}$
 $3\frac{1}{8}$
 $5\frac{1}{2}$

12. _____ (17)
13. _____ (17)
14. _____ (17)

85

Test 42

Name _____ **Total Score** _____
Date _____ **Basic Score** __100__
Basic Time — 8 Minutes **Improvement Score** _____

Add the whole-number portions and the fractional parts of each problem separately and then combine the results. Place each answer in the appropriate space on the right.

1. $4\frac{3}{4}$
    $7\frac{1}{2}$

2. $6\frac{2}{3}$
    $9\frac{5}{6}$

3. $8\frac{1}{6}$
    $5\frac{7}{12}$

4. $3\frac{1}{2}$
    $2\frac{1}{3}$

1. _____ (12)
2. _____ (12)
3. _____ (12)
4. _____ (12)

5. $6\frac{1}{2}$
    $12\frac{2}{3}$

6. $7\frac{1}{2}$
    $8\frac{1}{5}$

7. $8\frac{3}{4}$
    $12\frac{5}{6}$

8. $7\frac{3}{16}$
    $8\frac{5}{9}$

5. _____ (14)
6. _____ (14)
7. _____ (14)
8. _____ (14)

9. $14\frac{3}{8}$
    $17\frac{2}{3}$

10. $75\frac{2}{5}$
    $14\frac{3}{8}$

11. $16\frac{19}{24}$
    $32\frac{15}{32}$

9. _____ (15)
10. _____ (15)
11. _____ (15)

12. $3\frac{1}{3}$
    $1\frac{5}{8}$
    $4\frac{1}{2}$

13. $3\frac{2}{3}$
    $4\frac{1}{9}$
    $5\frac{1}{8}$

14. $9\frac{2}{3}$
    $4\frac{1}{5}$
    $6\frac{1}{2}$

12. _____ (17)
13. _____ (17)
14. _____ (17)

Exercise 43 — Subtraction of Common Fractions

When common fractions are to be subtracted, (1) change the fractions to equivalent fractions with common denominators; (2) find the difference between the numerators of the equivalent fractions; (3) place the difference over the common denominator; and (4) if necessary, reduce the answer to lowest terms. See these steps in the example.

Subtract: $\dfrac{9}{10} - \dfrac{1}{6} =$

Solution: $\dfrac{27}{30} - \dfrac{5}{30} = \dfrac{22}{30} = \dfrac{11}{15}$

Step 1   Steps 2, 3   Step 4

BASIC TIME — 9 Minutes *(Estimated time to obtain a basic score of 100)*

Subtract. Place each answer in the appropriate space on the right.

1. $\dfrac{3}{4} - \dfrac{2}{3} =$
2. $\dfrac{2}{3} - \dfrac{1}{2} =$
3. $\dfrac{7}{8} - \dfrac{2}{3} =$
4. $\dfrac{2}{3} - \dfrac{3}{8} =$
5. $\dfrac{4}{5} - \dfrac{3}{8} =$
6. $\dfrac{4}{5} - \dfrac{5}{12} =$
7. $\dfrac{9}{10} - \dfrac{2}{3} =$
8. $\dfrac{1}{3} - \dfrac{5}{16} =$
9. $\dfrac{5}{6} - \dfrac{5}{8} =$
10. $\dfrac{4}{5} - \dfrac{3}{4} =$
11. $\dfrac{15}{16} - \dfrac{2}{5} =$
12. $\dfrac{5}{9} - \dfrac{3}{8} =$
13. $\dfrac{6}{7} - \dfrac{5}{9} =$
14. $\dfrac{9}{16} - \dfrac{5}{12} =$
15. $\dfrac{24}{25} - \dfrac{24}{35} =$
16. $\dfrac{15}{18} - \dfrac{19}{24} =$

1. _____(10)
2. _____(10)
3. _____(10)
4. _____(10)
5. _____(10)
6. _____(10)
7. _____(10)
8. _____(10)
9. _____(10)
10. _____(10)
11. _____(15)
12. _____(15)
13. _____(15)
14. _____(15)
15. _____(20)
16. _____(20)

Test 43

Name _____ Total Score _____
Date _____ Basic Score __100__
Basic Time — 8 Minutes Improvement Score _____

Subtract. Place each answer in the appropriate space on the right.

1. $\dfrac{1}{2} - \dfrac{1}{3} =$ 2. $\dfrac{2}{3} - \dfrac{1}{4} =$

3. $\dfrac{3}{4} - \dfrac{1}{6} =$ 4. $\dfrac{5}{6} - \dfrac{2}{5} =$

5. $\dfrac{5}{8} - \dfrac{3}{7} =$ 6. $\dfrac{6}{7} - \dfrac{3}{5} =$

7. $\dfrac{7}{8} - \dfrac{5}{6} =$ 8. $\dfrac{4}{7} - \dfrac{1}{8} =$

9. $\dfrac{5}{6} - \dfrac{5}{8} =$ 10. $\dfrac{7}{12} - \dfrac{3}{8} =$

11. $\dfrac{5}{6} - \dfrac{5}{16} =$ 12. $\dfrac{7}{8} - \dfrac{2}{3} =$

13. $\dfrac{6}{7} - \dfrac{4}{5} =$ 14. $\dfrac{8}{9} - \dfrac{4}{11} =$

15. $\dfrac{9}{10} - \dfrac{1}{6} =$ 16. $\dfrac{11}{16} - \dfrac{2}{3} =$

1. _____ (10)
2. _____ (10)
3. _____ (10)
4. _____ (10)
5. _____ (12)
6. _____ (12)
7. _____ (12)
8. _____ (12)
9. _____ (12)
10. _____ (12)
11. _____ (14)
12. _____ (14)
13. _____ (15)
14. _____ (15)
15. _____ (15)
16. _____ (15)

Exercise 44 Subtraction of Mixed Numbers

When mixed numbers are to be subtracted, (1) change each mixed number to an improper fraction; (2) convert the improper fractions to equivalent fractions with common denominators; (3) subtract the numerators; (4) place the difference over the common denominator; and (5) if necessary, reduce to lowest terms or a mixed number. See these steps in the example.

Subtract: $5\frac{1}{3} - 3\frac{1}{2} =$

Solution:

$\frac{16}{3} - \frac{7}{2} = \frac{32}{6} - \frac{21}{6} = \frac{11}{6} = 1\frac{5}{6}$

Step 1   Step 2   Steps 3, 4   Step 5

BASIC TIME — 12 Minutes *(Estimated time to obtain a basic score of 100)*

Subtract. Place each answer in the appropriate space on the right.

1. $5\frac{3}{4} - 3\frac{1}{4} =$
2. $12\frac{2}{3} - 7\frac{1}{3} =$
3. $3\frac{1}{2} - 1\frac{1}{4} =$
4. $3\frac{1}{8} - 2\frac{1}{2} =$
5. $7\frac{3}{16} - 5\frac{5}{8} =$
6. $7\frac{2}{3} - 3\frac{4}{5} =$
7. $6\frac{3}{4} - 5\frac{5}{9} =$
8. $4\frac{1}{3} - 3\frac{1}{2} =$
9. $7\frac{3}{4} - 5\frac{1}{6} =$
10. $9\frac{3}{5} - 7\frac{1}{2} =$
11. $12\frac{1}{8} - 11\frac{7}{12} =$
12. $13\frac{4}{5} - 9\frac{1}{6} =$
13. $32\frac{1}{8} - 25\frac{1}{12} =$
14. $14\frac{2}{3} - 8\frac{7}{8} =$
15. $35\frac{4}{9} - 18\frac{1}{6} =$
16. $62\frac{5}{12} - 6\frac{1}{5} =$

1. _____(10)
2. _____(10)
3. _____(10)
4. _____(10)
5. _____(12)
6. _____(12)
7. _____(12)
8. _____(12)
9. _____(12)
10. _____(12)
11. _____(14)
12. _____(14)
13. _____(15)
14. _____(15)
15. _____(15)
16. _____(15)

Test 44

Name _____ Total Score _____

Date _____ Basic Score __100__

Basic Time — 10 Minutes   Improvement Score _____

Subtract. Place each answer in the appropriate space on the right.

1. $7\frac{1}{2} - 1\frac{1}{4} =$

2. $6\frac{2}{3} - 3\frac{1}{6} =$

3. $10\frac{7}{8} - 6\frac{3}{4} =$

4. $9\frac{11}{16} - 7\frac{3}{4} =$

5. $4\frac{7}{8} - 2\frac{3}{5} =$

6. $6\frac{7}{8} - 4\frac{1}{6} =$

7. $5\frac{1}{6} - 2\frac{3}{4} =$

8. $9\frac{4}{5} - 8\frac{2}{3} =$

9. $7\frac{2}{5} - 6\frac{1}{4} =$

10. $16\frac{1}{3} - 7\frac{1}{8} =$

11. $3\frac{1}{3} - 2\frac{1}{2} =$

12. $6\frac{2}{3} - 5\frac{5}{8} =$

13. $9\frac{2}{3} - 8\frac{4}{5} =$

14. $12\frac{3}{4} - 5\frac{5}{6} =$

15. $12\frac{1}{4} - 8\frac{1}{3} =$

16. $15\frac{1}{2} - 12\frac{1}{8} =$

1. _____ (10)
2. _____ (10)
3. _____ (10)
4. _____ (10)
5. _____ (12)
6. _____ (12)
7. _____ (12)
8. _____ (12)
9. _____ (12)
10. _____ (12)
11. _____ (14)
12. _____ (14)
13. _____ (15)
14. _____ (15)
15. _____ (15)
16. _____ (15)

Exercise 45 — Multiplication of Common Fractions

To multiply common fractions, see Example A.

Example A $\quad \dfrac{7}{8} \times \dfrac{5}{6} = \dfrac{7 \times 5}{8 \times 6} = \dfrac{35}{48}$

Solution A. Multiply the numerators, giving 7 × 5 = 35, the numerator of the result. Multiply the denominators, giving 8 × 6 = 48, the denominator of the result.

To divide the numerators and denominators by common divisors before multiplying common fractions, see Example B.

Example B $\quad \dfrac{3}{8} \times \dfrac{5}{6} \times \dfrac{4}{5} = \dfrac{\overset{1}{\cancel{3}}}{\underset{2}{\cancel{8}}} \times \dfrac{\overset{1}{\cancel{5}}}{\underset{2}{\cancel{6}}} \times \dfrac{\overset{1}{\cancel{4}}}{\underset{1}{\cancel{5}}} = \dfrac{1}{4}$

Solution B. Divide any numerator and denominator by a common divisor. In Example B the 3 in the first numerator and the 6 in the second denominator have a common divisor of 3. Dividing by 3 leaves a 1 and 2 respectively. The 4 in the third numerator and the 8 in the first denominator may be divided by 4 leaving 1 and 2 respectively. The 5 in the second numerator and 5 in the third denominator may be divided by 5 leaving a 1 in both places. Multiply the numerators (1 × 1 × 1) giving 1 in the numerator of the result. Multiply the denominators (2 × 2 × 1) giving 4 in the denominator of the result. When the numerators and denominators have no common divisors, proceed as in Example A.

BASIC TIME — 5 Minutes *(Estimated time to obtain a basic score of 100)*

Multiply:

1. $\dfrac{3}{8} \times \dfrac{3}{5} =$
2. $\dfrac{5}{9} \times \dfrac{7}{12} =$
3. $\dfrac{4}{5} \times \dfrac{2}{3} =$ (6)

4. $\dfrac{5}{16} \times \dfrac{7}{8} =$
5. $\dfrac{2}{3} \times \dfrac{16}{25} =$
6. $\dfrac{2}{9} \times \dfrac{7}{11} =$ (6)

7. $\dfrac{15}{16} \times \dfrac{3}{4} =$
8. $\dfrac{9}{10} \times \dfrac{7}{8} =$
9. $\dfrac{11}{12} \times \dfrac{5}{16} =$ (6)

10. $\dfrac{19}{24} \times \dfrac{5}{6} =$
11. $\dfrac{3}{5} \times \dfrac{3}{16} =$
12. $\dfrac{7}{12} \times \dfrac{5}{8} =$ (6)

13. $\dfrac{7}{8} \times \dfrac{6}{7} =$
14. $\dfrac{5}{9} \times \dfrac{9}{10} =$
15. $\dfrac{4}{5} \times \dfrac{5}{8} =$ (6)

16. $\dfrac{15}{16} \times \dfrac{32}{45} =$
17. $\dfrac{7}{16} \times \dfrac{4}{5} =$
18. $\dfrac{5}{16} \times \dfrac{4}{15} =$ (6)

19. $\dfrac{3}{8} \times \dfrac{4}{5} \times \dfrac{5}{9} \times \dfrac{2}{3} =$
20. $\dfrac{9}{10} \times \dfrac{5}{12} \times \dfrac{16}{21} \times \dfrac{3}{4} =$ (10)

21. $\dfrac{3}{16} \times \dfrac{4}{5} \times \dfrac{2}{3} \times \dfrac{1}{4} =$
22. $\dfrac{7}{8} \times \dfrac{2}{3} \times \dfrac{1}{2} \times \dfrac{5}{7} =$ (10)

23. $\dfrac{5}{12} \times \dfrac{7}{16} \times \dfrac{8}{15} \times \dfrac{16}{21} =$
24. $\dfrac{4}{5} \times \dfrac{5}{7} \times \dfrac{7}{8} \times \dfrac{1}{2} =$ (12)

25. $\dfrac{13}{15} \times \dfrac{5}{12} \times \dfrac{8}{9} \times \dfrac{3}{4} =$
26. $\dfrac{7}{9} \times \dfrac{5}{12} \times \dfrac{3}{14} \times \dfrac{3}{5} =$ (14)

Test 45

Name _____
Date _____
Basic Time — 2½ Minutes

Total Score _____
Basic Score   100
Improvement Score _____

Multiply. Place each answer in the appropriate space on the right.

1. $\dfrac{5}{6} \times \dfrac{7}{8} =$ 2. $\dfrac{3}{5} \times \dfrac{4}{5} =$

3. $\dfrac{7}{16} \times \dfrac{5}{12} =$ 4. $\dfrac{4}{5} \times \dfrac{5}{8} =$

5. $\dfrac{3}{4} \times \dfrac{5}{12} =$ 6. $\dfrac{7}{8} \times \dfrac{6}{7} =$

7. $\dfrac{2}{3} \times \dfrac{7}{8} =$ 8. $\dfrac{9}{16} \times \dfrac{8}{9} =$

9. $\dfrac{4}{9} \times \dfrac{3}{4} =$ 10. $\dfrac{7}{15} \times \dfrac{24}{35} =$

11. $\dfrac{2}{3} \times \dfrac{4}{5} \times \dfrac{5}{8} =$

12. $\dfrac{3}{8} \times \dfrac{11}{12} \times \dfrac{16}{33} =$

13. $\dfrac{7}{8} \times \dfrac{3}{5} \times \dfrac{5}{7} \times \dfrac{4}{5} \times \dfrac{2}{3} =$

14. $\dfrac{7}{16} \times \dfrac{8}{9} \times \dfrac{2}{7} \times \dfrac{5}{6} \times \dfrac{1}{2} =$

15. $\dfrac{1}{5} \times \dfrac{2}{3} \times \dfrac{5}{12} \times \dfrac{6}{7} \times \dfrac{7}{8} =$

1. _____ (8)
2. _____ (8)
3. _____ (8)
4. _____ (8)
5. _____ (8)
6. _____ (8)
7. _____ (8)
8. _____ (8)
9. _____ (8)
10. _____ (12)
11. _____ (12)
12. _____ (18)
13. _____ (28)
14. _____ (30)
15. _____ (28)

Exercise 46 — Multiplication of Mixed Numbers

To multiply mixed numbers, change each mixed number to its equivalent improper fraction. Then multiply in the manner described in Exercise 45. If possible, use cancellation by dividing the numerators and denominators by common divisors before proceeding with the multiplication. See the example at the right.

Multiply:

$$1\tfrac{2}{5} \times 3\tfrac{1}{3} \times 1\tfrac{1}{7} = \frac{\cancel{7}^{1}}{\cancel{5}_{1}} \times \frac{\cancel{10}^{2}}{3} \times \frac{8}{\cancel{7}_{1}} = \frac{16}{3} = 5\tfrac{1}{3}$$

BASIC TIME — 10 Minutes *(Estimated time to obtain a basic score of 100)*

Multiply. Place each answer in the appropriate space on the right.

1. $3\tfrac{1}{2} \times 4\tfrac{2}{3} =$
2. $5\tfrac{1}{4} \times 2\tfrac{1}{3} =$
3. $7\tfrac{3}{8} \times 9\tfrac{5}{6} =$
4. $8\tfrac{5}{9} \times 4\tfrac{1}{11} =$
5. $12\tfrac{1}{5} \times 10\tfrac{5}{9} =$
6. $6\tfrac{5}{8} \times 12\tfrac{6}{7} =$
7. $17\tfrac{1}{2} \times 19\tfrac{1}{5} =$
8. $14\tfrac{2}{7} \times 16\tfrac{3}{5} =$
9. $23\tfrac{4}{7} \times 19\tfrac{5}{8} =$
10. $35\tfrac{7}{16} \times 24\tfrac{5}{12} =$
11. $28\tfrac{11}{12} \times 15\tfrac{5}{6} =$
12. $18\tfrac{8}{9} \times 26\tfrac{5}{7} =$

1. _____(15)
2. _____(15)
3. _____(15)
4. _____(15)
5. _____(15)
6. _____(15)
7. _____(15)
8. _____(15)
9. _____(20)
10. _____(20)
11. _____(20)
12. _____(20)

Test 46

Name _____ Total Score _____

Date _____ Basic Score ___100___

Basic Time — 10 Minutes   Improvement Score _____

Multiply. Place each answer in the appropriate space on the right.

1. $4\frac{2}{3} \times 6\frac{1}{2} =$ 2. $9\frac{3}{4} \times 10\frac{1}{3} =$

3. $5\frac{3}{8} \times 7\frac{2}{5} =$ 4. $8\frac{5}{6} \times 3\frac{2}{7} =$

5. $11\frac{5}{9} \times 6\frac{1}{12} =$ 6. $6\frac{7}{8} \times 4\frac{15}{16} =$

7. $12\frac{4}{7} \times 9\frac{7}{11} =$ 8. $15\frac{1}{3} \times 16\frac{2}{3} =$

9. $27\frac{5}{8} \times 19\frac{7}{12} =$

10. $16\frac{1}{8} \times 18\frac{5}{9} =$

11. $3\frac{24}{25} \times 5\frac{15}{16} =$

12. $8\frac{11}{12} \times 12\frac{7}{11} =$

1. _____(15)
2. _____(15)
3. _____(15)
4. _____(15)
5. _____(15)
6. _____(15)
7. _____(15)
8. _____(15)
9. _____(20)
10. _____(20)
11. _____(20)
12. _____(20)

Exercise 47 — Multiplication of Whole Numbers by Common Fractions

Any problem requiring multiplication of whole numbers by a common fraction may be interpreted to mean:

$$\frac{\text{Numerator} \times \text{Numerator}}{\text{Denominator} \times \text{Denominator}} = \text{Product}$$

In Example A below, the whole number 37 means 37 ones and may be written as $\frac{37}{1}$. Therefore, multiply the denominators, giving $1 \times 5 = 5$. Then reduce the resulting improper fraction to lowest terms.

Example A $37 \times \frac{1}{5} = \frac{37}{1} \times \frac{1}{5} = \frac{37}{5} = 7\frac{2}{5}$

You may be able to cancel by using common divisors. See Example B.

Example B $45 \times \frac{2}{3} = \frac{\cancel{45}^{15}}{1} \times \frac{2}{\cancel{3}_1} = \frac{30}{1} = 30$

If you cannot cancel easily, multiply the numerators. Then divide the result by the product of the denominators, and reduce to lowest terms. See Example C.

Example C $57 \times \frac{5}{6} = \frac{57}{1} \times \frac{5}{6} = \frac{285}{6} = 47\frac{3}{6} = 47\frac{1}{2}$

BASIC TIME — 9 Minutes *(Estimated time to obtain a basic score of 100)*

Multiply. Show each answer in lowest terms. Place each answer in the appropriate space on the right.

1. $130 \times \frac{1}{5} =$
2. $268 \times \frac{1}{4} =$
3. $178 \times \frac{1}{2} =$
4. $135 \times \frac{1}{3} =$
5. $168 \times \frac{1}{7} =$
6. $232 \times \frac{1}{8} =$
7. $277 \times \frac{1}{6} =$
8. $472 \times \frac{1}{9} =$
9. $\frac{1}{8} \times 387 =$
10. $\frac{1}{5} \times 367 =$
11. $\frac{3}{4} \times 76 =$
12. $186 \times \frac{2}{3} =$
13. $\frac{5}{6} \times 243 =$
14. $590 \times \frac{7}{8} =$
15. $\frac{12}{13} \times 68 =$
16. $57 \times \frac{15}{17} =$

1. _____(10)
2. _____(10)
3. _____(10)
4. _____(10)
5. _____(10)
6. _____(10)
7. _____(10)
8. _____(10)
9. _____(10)
10. _____(15)
11. _____(15)
12. _____(15)
13. _____(15)
14. _____(15)
15. _____(20)
16. _____(20)

Test 47

Name _____ Total Score _____
Date _____ Basic Score __100__
Basic Time — 9 Minutes Improvement Score _____

Multiply. Show each answer in lowest terms. Place each answer in the appropriate space on the right.

1. $48 \times \frac{1}{3} =$ 2. $346 \times \frac{1}{2} =$

3. $\frac{1}{5} \times 245 =$ 4. $304 \times \frac{1}{4} =$

5. $1,026 \times \frac{1}{6} =$ 6. $\frac{1}{7} \times 525 =$

7. $\frac{1}{9} \times 172 =$ 8. $680 \times \frac{1}{8} =$

9. $\frac{1}{7} \times 342 =$ 10. $99 \times \frac{1}{6} =$

11. $810 \times \frac{2}{3} =$ 12. $\frac{3}{4} \times 743 =$

13. $\frac{5}{7} \times 244 =$ 14. $325 \times \frac{7}{8} =$

15. $172 \times \frac{11}{12} =$ 16. $108 \times \frac{13}{15} =$

1. _____ (10)
2. _____ (10)
3. _____ (10)
4. _____ (10)
5. _____ (10)
6. _____ (10)
7. _____ (10)
8. _____ (10)
9. _____ (10)
10. _____ (10)
11. _____ (15)
12. _____ (15)
13. _____ (15)
14. _____ (15)
15. _____ (20)
16. _____ (20)

Exercise 48 — Division of Common Fractions

To divide one common fraction by another, invert the divisor (that is, turn it upside down) and then multiply the fractions as described in Exercise 45. Reduce the quotient to lowest terms or a mixed number, if necessary.

See the example at the right, where $\frac{3}{4}$ is divided by $\frac{2}{3}$. Note that the divisor $\frac{2}{3}$ is inverted to $\frac{3}{2}$ and the division sign is changed to a multiplication sign. The two fractions are then multiplied, and the quotient reduced to a mixed number.

Divide: $\frac{3}{4} \div \frac{2}{3} = \frac{3}{4} \times \frac{3}{2} = \frac{9}{8} = 1\frac{1}{8}$

BASIC TIME — 3 Minutes *(Estimated time to obtain a basic score of 100)*

Divide. Place each answer in the appropriate space on the right.

1. $\dfrac{5}{8} \div \dfrac{2}{7} =$
2. $\dfrac{5}{12} \div \dfrac{7}{8} =$
3. $\dfrac{7}{15} \div \dfrac{4}{9} =$
4. $\dfrac{3}{16} \div \dfrac{1}{8} =$
5. $\dfrac{5}{9} \div \dfrac{7}{8} =$
6. $\dfrac{9}{16} \div \dfrac{7}{12} =$
7. $\dfrac{11}{12} \div \dfrac{14}{15} =$
8. $\dfrac{17}{18} \div \dfrac{8}{9} =$
9. $\dfrac{19}{32} \div \dfrac{17}{24} =$
10. $\dfrac{22}{27} \div \dfrac{28}{33} =$
11. $\dfrac{25}{42} \div \dfrac{5}{21} =$
12. $\dfrac{35}{72} \div \dfrac{21}{32} =$
13. $\dfrac{51}{56} \div \dfrac{17}{24} =$
14. $\dfrac{16}{25} \div \dfrac{36}{55} =$

1. _____ (10)
2. _____ (10)
3. _____ (10)
4. _____ (10)
5. _____ (12)
6. _____ (12)
7. _____ (12)
8. _____ (12)
9. _____ (18)
10. _____ (18)
11. _____ (18)
12. _____ (18)
13. _____ (20)
14. _____ (20)

98

Test 48

Name _____ Total Score _____
Date _____ Basic Score __100__
Basic Time — 3 Minutes Improvement Score _____

Divide. Place each answer in the appropriate space on the right.

1. $\dfrac{4}{5} \div \dfrac{7}{8} =$
2. $\dfrac{5}{16} \div \dfrac{4}{15} =$

3. $\dfrac{11}{12} \div \dfrac{15}{16} =$
4. $\dfrac{5}{9} \div \dfrac{7}{11} =$

5. $\dfrac{9}{16} \div \dfrac{5}{12} =$
6. $\dfrac{17}{24} \div \dfrac{19}{32} =$

7. $\dfrac{16}{21} \div \dfrac{8}{9} =$
8. $\dfrac{27}{32} \div \dfrac{9}{16} =$

9. $\dfrac{24}{25} \div \dfrac{32}{45} =$
10. $\dfrac{62}{63} \div \dfrac{31}{42} =$

11. $\dfrac{18}{25} \div \dfrac{9}{10} =$
12. $\dfrac{25}{27} \div \dfrac{17}{18} =$

13. $\dfrac{13}{22} \div \dfrac{23}{25} =$
14. $\dfrac{29}{36} \div \dfrac{18}{19} =$

1. _____ (10)
2. _____ (10)
3. _____ (10)
4. _____ (10)
5. _____ (12)
6. _____ (12)
7. _____ (12)
8. _____ (12)
9. _____ (18)
10. _____ (18)
11. _____ (18)
12. _____ (18)
13. _____ (20)
14. _____ (20)

Exercise 49 — Division of Mixed Numbers

To divide one mixed number by another, change each mixed number to an improper fraction. Then proceed as in the division of common fractions described in Exercise 48.

Divide: $3\frac{2}{3} \div 2\frac{1}{2} = \frac{11}{3} \div \frac{5}{2} = \frac{11}{3} \times \frac{2}{5} = \frac{22}{15} = 1\frac{7}{15}$

BASIC TIME — 7 Minutes *(Estimated time to obtain a basic score of 100)*

Divide. Place each answer in the appropriate space on the right.

1. $5\frac{1}{2} \div 3\frac{1}{3} =$
2. $6\frac{3}{4} \div 5\frac{1}{2} =$
3. $3\frac{3}{5} \div 5\frac{1}{4} =$
4. $7\frac{2}{3} \div 2\frac{3}{4} =$
5. $8\frac{5}{6} \div 6\frac{2}{3} =$
6. $2\frac{3}{8} \div 4\frac{1}{6} =$
7. $13\frac{5}{8} \div 7\frac{1}{8} =$
8. $12\frac{5}{7} \div 15\frac{4}{5} =$
9. $32\frac{11}{35} \div 19\frac{17}{20} =$
10. $24\frac{9}{10} \div 7\frac{15}{44} =$
11. $64\frac{1}{2} \div 24\frac{1}{3} =$
12. $16\frac{1}{4} \div 8\frac{1}{3} =$

1. _____(12)
2. _____(12)
3. _____(12)
4. _____(12)
5. _____(16)
6. _____(16)
7. _____(16)
8. _____(16)
9. _____(22)
10. _____(22)
11. _____(22)
12. _____(22)

Test 49

Name _____ Total Score _____
Date _____ Basic Score 100
Basic Time — 5 Minutes Improvement Score _____

Divide. Place each answer in the appropriate space on the right.

1. $2\frac{3}{8} \div 1\frac{3}{4} =$

2. $7\frac{1}{2} \div 5\frac{2}{3} =$

3. $9\frac{3}{5} \div 6\frac{1}{4} =$

4. $12\frac{2}{5} \div 9\frac{5}{6} =$

5. $10\frac{5}{8} \div 5\frac{5}{6} =$

6. $8\frac{4}{5} \div 16\frac{2}{3} =$

7. $25\frac{4}{9} \div 12\frac{5}{6} =$

8. $32\frac{3}{5} \div 21\frac{3}{4} =$

9. $19\frac{13}{16} \div 22\frac{7}{8} =$

10. $24\frac{19}{25} \div 16\frac{47}{75} =$

11. $16\frac{3}{8} \div 17\frac{5}{12} =$

12. $31\frac{5}{9} \div 25\frac{2}{3} =$

13. $27\frac{6}{7} \div 9\frac{2}{3} =$

14. $14\frac{2}{7} \div 24\frac{9}{14} =$

1. _____ (10)
2. _____ (10)
3. _____ (10)
4. _____ (10)
5. _____ (12)
6. _____ (12)
7. _____ (12)
8. _____ (12)
9. _____ (18)
10. _____ (18)
11. _____ (18)
12. _____ (18)
13. _____ (20)
14. _____ (20)

Exercise 50: Simplification of Complex Fractions

A fraction that has a fraction or a mixed number, or both, for its numerator or denominator is a **complex fraction**. In a common fraction, both the numerator and denominator (dividend and divisor) are whole numbers. The line between the numerator and the denominator of a fraction, whether common or complex, is simply one way of showing division. When a complex fraction has been reduced to lowest terms, it is said to have been *simplified*.

To simplify a complex fraction, perform the division indicated, following the rules for division of common fractions. Remember that 1 is understood to be the denominator of a whole number.

Simplify: $\dfrac{5\frac{1}{4}}{6} = 5\frac{1}{4} \div 6 = \dfrac{\cancel{21}^{7}}{4} \times \dfrac{1}{\cancel{6}_{2}} = \dfrac{7}{8}$

BASIC TIME — 6 Minutes *(Estimated time to obtain a basic score of 100)*

Simplify these complex fractions. Place each answer in the appropriate space on the right. (20 each)

1. $\dfrac{5}{\frac{3}{4}} =$

2. $\dfrac{6\frac{1}{2}}{8\frac{1}{4}} =$

3. $\dfrac{16\frac{2}{3}}{100} =$

4. $\dfrac{\frac{5}{6}}{7\frac{1}{2}} =$

5. $\dfrac{\frac{2}{3}}{\frac{5}{6}} =$

6. $\dfrac{3\frac{2}{3}}{9\frac{3}{4}} =$

7. $\dfrac{\frac{1}{4}}{\frac{7}{8}} =$

8. $\dfrac{10\frac{4}{5}}{12\frac{5}{8}} =$

9. $\dfrac{\frac{3}{5}}{\frac{4}{7}} =$

10. $\dfrac{87\frac{1}{2}}{100} =$

1. _____
2. _____
3. _____
4. _____
5. _____
6. _____
7. _____
8. _____
9. _____
10. _____

Test 50

Name _____ Total Score _____

Date _____ Basic Score __100__

Basic Time — 5 Minutes Improvement Score _____

Simplify these complex fractions. Place each answer in the appropriate space on the right. (20 each)

1. $\dfrac{12\frac{1}{2}}{100} =$

2. $\dfrac{12\frac{1}{5}}{7\frac{1}{2}} =$

3. $\dfrac{\frac{1}{7}}{10} =$

4. $\dfrac{9\frac{5}{12}}{12\frac{3}{4}} =$

5. $\dfrac{3\frac{1}{3}}{10} =$

6. $\dfrac{7\frac{2}{3}}{34\frac{5}{9}} =$

7. $\dfrac{9}{\frac{3}{4}} =$

8. $\dfrac{5\frac{1}{4}}{16\frac{4}{5}} =$

9. $\dfrac{\frac{5}{8}}{\frac{5}{6}} =$

10. $\dfrac{27\frac{1}{3}}{36\frac{3}{4}} =$

1. _____
2. _____
3. _____
4. _____
5. _____
6. _____
7. _____
8. _____
9. _____
10. _____

Exercise 51 — Review of Fractions

This lesson is a review of fractions. Whenever possible, use one of the short methods presented in the preceding exercises. In any case, use the method that gives you the greatest accuracy.

BASIC TIME — 7 Minutes *(Estimated time to obtain a basic score of 100)*

Solve these problems. Place each answer in the appropriate space on the right.

Change to lowest terms:

1. $\dfrac{64}{160} =$
2. $\dfrac{90}{135} =$

Add:

3. $\dfrac{3}{4} + \dfrac{5}{6} + \dfrac{7}{8} =$
4. $16\dfrac{2}{3} + 12\dfrac{5}{16} =$

Find the difference:

5. $\dfrac{11}{12} - \dfrac{7}{8} =$
6. $15\dfrac{2}{3} - 12\dfrac{3}{4} =$

Multiply:

7. $\dfrac{3}{4} \times \dfrac{5}{16} \times \dfrac{1}{2} =$
8. $\dfrac{9}{16} \times \dfrac{2}{3} \times \dfrac{7}{8} \times \dfrac{5}{7} =$
9. $18\dfrac{3}{4} \times 6\dfrac{2}{3} =$
10. $25\dfrac{5}{12} \times 15\dfrac{3}{8} =$

Divide:

11. $\dfrac{3}{8} \div \dfrac{5}{12} =$
12. $\dfrac{7}{16} \div \dfrac{7}{12} =$
13. $6\dfrac{2}{3} \div 12\dfrac{1}{2} =$
14. $18\dfrac{3}{4} \div 5\dfrac{5}{6} =$

1. _____ (10)
2. _____ (10)
3. _____ (10)
4. _____ (10)
5. _____ (12)
6. _____ (12)
7. _____ (12)
8. _____ (12)
9. _____ (18)
10. _____ (18)
11. _____ (18)
12. _____ (18)
13. _____ (20)
14. _____ (20)

Test 51

Name _____ Total Score _____

Date _____ Basic Score __100__

Basic Time — 9 Minutes Improvement Score _____

Solve these problems. Place each answer in the appropriate space on the right.

Add:

1. $\frac{1}{2} + \frac{1}{3} + \frac{1}{4} + \frac{1}{6} =$

2. $\frac{3}{4} + \frac{5}{6} + \frac{7}{8} + \frac{5}{12} =$

3. $16\frac{2}{3} + \frac{7}{16} + 5\frac{3}{4} =$

4. $9\frac{5}{6} + 7\frac{7}{16} + 3\frac{11}{18} =$

Find the difference:

5. $\frac{5}{12} - \frac{3}{16} =$

6. $\frac{13}{16} - \frac{11}{24} =$

7. $17\frac{7}{8} - 9\frac{1}{3} =$

8. $12\frac{1}{2} - 8\frac{8}{9} =$

Multiply:

9. $\frac{15}{16} \times \frac{23}{32} =$

10. $\frac{3}{4} \times \frac{5}{6} \times \frac{7}{8} =$

11. $16\frac{2}{3} \times 12\frac{1}{2} =$

12. $17\frac{11}{12} \times 6\frac{7}{16} =$

Divide:

13. $\frac{63}{64} \div \frac{9}{16} =$

14. $35\frac{7}{12} \div 16\frac{2}{3} =$

1. _____ (10)
2. _____ (10)
3. _____ (10)
4. _____ (10)
5. _____ (12)
6. _____ (12)
7. _____ (12)
8. _____ (12)
9. _____ (18)
10. _____ (18)
11. _____ (18)
12. _____ (18)
13. _____ (20)
14. _____ (20)

Exercise 52 Application Problems

BASIC TIME — 8 Minutes *(Estimated time to obtain a basic score of 100)*

Solve these problems. Place each answer in the appropriate space on the right. (20 each)

1. Phil weighs $226\frac{5}{6}$ pounds when wearing all of his scuba gear, which weighs $54\frac{1}{2}$ pounds. How much does Phil weigh without the scuba gear? .... _____

2. Which problem has the larger sum: (a) $\frac{3}{8} + \frac{2}{9} + \frac{5}{6}$ or (b) $\frac{1}{9} + \frac{3}{5} + \frac{7}{10}$? How much larger? .... _____

3. A homeowner plans to place some 12-inch boards, on shelf brackets in the kitchen to make 2 shelves $4\frac{3}{4}$ feet long and 4 shelves $3\frac{1}{3}$ feet long. How many feet of 12-inch boards are needed for these shelves? .... _____

4. A farmer harvested 56 of the 72 acres that were planted in corn. What fractional part of the corn crop was harvested? .... _____

5. It is $\frac{3}{4}$ mile from the cabin to the lake. Four people each carried the boat oars $\frac{1}{4}$ of the way to the lake. What fractional part of a mile did each person carry the oars?. _____

6. Last year Jeanne's salary was $18,000. This year her salary is $\frac{3}{20}$ more. How much is her salary this year? .... _____

7. A caterer who has 4 large cakes wishes to serve 48 equal portions. Each portion will be what fractional part of a cake? .... _____

8. Don had a difficult time rowing up a swift stream. He rowed at a rate of $\frac{3}{5}$ mile an hour. At this rate, how long did it take him to row $3\frac{1}{3}$ miles? .... _____

9. Diane drove 18 miles from her house. This was $\frac{2}{3}$ of the distance she had to drive in order to reach the theater. How many miles did she have to drive from her house to reach the theater? .... _____

10. How many pies are needed to serve $\frac{1}{6}$ pie to each of 54 guests? .... _____

Test 52

Name _____ Total Score _____

Date _____ Basic Score __100__

Basic Time — 7 Minutes Improvement Score _____

Solve these problems. Write the answers in the spaces on the right. (20 each)

1. A company's stock sold at $95\tfrac{3}{8}$ per share when the stock market opened for the day. The stock sold for $92\tfrac{5}{8}$ when the stock market closed that day. How many points per share did this stock drop that day?.. _____

2. In order to expand its runways, an airport bought five tracts of land: $62\tfrac{5}{6}$ acres, $14\tfrac{4}{5}$ acres, $33\tfrac{2}{3}$ acres, $49\tfrac{7}{15}$ acres, and $10\tfrac{3}{5}$ acres. How many acres did the airport purchase?... _____

3. Norman bought half of a watermelon. He shared it with three friends. If Norman divided the watermelon equally, what part of a whole watermelon did each person receive?.. _____

4. The Garcia family spent $\tfrac{1}{5}$ of its income for rent, $\tfrac{1}{4}$ for food, $\tfrac{1}{3}$ for clothing, $\tfrac{1}{6}$ for miscellaneous items, and saved the remainder. What fractional part of the income was saved? .... _____

5. A delivery truck averages $13\tfrac{3}{4}$ miles per gallon of gasoline. How many gallons of gasoline were used to drive this truck $1{,}098\tfrac{9}{10}$ miles? .... _____

6. If a pilot flew a plane 555 miles in $1\tfrac{5}{6}$ hours, what was the average speed per hour? .... _____

7. How many pieces of fabric $3\tfrac{1}{3}$ yards long can be cut from a bolt of fabric that is 40 yards long? .... _____

8. A farmer sold $62\tfrac{1}{2}$ acres of a 750-acre farm. Expressed as a fraction, what part of the farm was sold?.. _____

9. A water tank held $719\tfrac{3}{4}$ gallons. If 18 barrels, each containing $37\tfrac{1}{2}$ gallons, were drawn from it, how many gallons would remain in the tank?........................... _____

10. The partnership of Lee, Cohen, and O'Hara agreed to share gains and losses in proportion to their respective investments. Lee invested $21,000; Cohen, $35,000; and O'Hara, $28,000. If they are to share a net gain of $21,600, how much should (a) Lee, (b) Cohen, and (c) O'Hara receive?..............................

(a) _____

(b) _____

(c) _____

Exercise 53 Rounding Numbers

In order to round any number to a specific place, you must remember only two rules. (1) Select the desired place (such as the nearest thousand or nearest million) and omit all numerals to the right of that place, substituting 0's. (2) If the first numeral in the part omitted (shown in parentheses in Example A) is (a) 5 or greater, increase the preceding numeral by 1 or (b) 4 or smaller, keep the preceding numeral the same.

Example A   Round 4,756,875 to nearest hundred thousand:

4,7(56,875)   part to be omitted in parentheses
+1   part omitted starts with 5; add 1 to the 7
4,8 00,000   0's substituted in rounded number

Example B   Round 73,432 to nearest thousand:

73,(432)   part to be omitted in parentheses
0   part omitted starts with 4; add 0 to the 3
73, 000   0's substituted in rounded number

Follow these rules to round decimal fractions except do not substitute 0's for the part omitted.

Example C   Round 519.072364 to nearest ten thousandth (4th decimal place):

519.0723(64)   part to be omitted in parentheses
+ 1   part omitted starts with 6; add 1 to the 3
519.0724   0's **not** substituted

You should perform these processes mentally, writing only the rounded number.

BASIC TIME — 3 Minutes *(Estimated time to obtain a basic score of 100)*

Round the following numbers to the places indicated: (10 each)

1. 264 to nearest ten ....
2. 267 to nearest ten ....
3. 7,400 to nearest thousand ....
4. 2,060 to nearest hundred ....
5. 21,220 to nearest hundred ....
6. 882,650 to nearest thousand ....
7. 518,660 to nearest thousand ....
8. 104,746 to nearest ten thousand ....
9. 207,614 to nearest ten thousand ....
10. 7,880,000 to nearest hundred thousand ....
11. 4,460,132,158 to nearest hundred million ....
12. 62,059,800,000 to nearest million ....
13. 103,097,356,226 to nearest ten million ....
14. 1,026,844,671,486 to nearest billion ....
15. 2,122.770263 to nearest tenth (1st decimal place) ....
16. 778.45435 to nearest hundredth (2d decimal place) ....
17. 107.10614 to nearest thousandth (3d decimal place) ....
18. 33.9088623 to nearest ten thousandth (4th decimal place) ....
19. 7.752632 to nearest hundred thousandth (5th decimal place) ....
20. 23.0807140723 to nearest millionth (6th decimal place) ....

Test 53

Name _____ Total Score _____

Date _____ Basic Score ___100___

Basic Time — 3 Minutes Improvement Score _____

Round the following numbers to the places indicated: (10 each)

1. 2,008 to nearest ten .... _____

2. 2,024 to nearest ten .... _____

3. 1,710 to nearest hundred .... _____

4. 3,761 to nearest hundred .... _____

5. 89,108 to nearest thousand .... _____

6. 172,837 to nearest thousand .... _____

7. 313,866,334 to nearest million .... _____

8. 734,196,855,447 to nearest ten million .... _____

9. 43,588,588 to nearest ten thousand .... _____

10. 53,716,240 to nearest ten million .... _____

11. 190,897,794,295 to nearest billion .... _____

12. 46,823,462,770 to nearest hundred thousand .... _____

13. 211,867,752,000 to nearest hundred million .... _____

14. 324,621,720.351251 to nearest hundredth .... _____

15. 434,750,004.780347 to nearest ten thousandth .... _____

16. 3,976.870261663 to nearest millionth .... _____

17. 3,976.780871 to nearest hundred thousandth .... _____

18. 20,645.623103 to nearest tenth .... _____

19. 345.8875768642 to nearest millionth .... _____

20. 5,930.813206584 to nearest ten thousandth .... _____

Exercise 54 — Equivalent Decimal and Common Fractions

Study these examples that show how to change common fractions to equivalent decimal fractions and decimal fractions to common fractions.

Example A $\quad \dfrac{1}{2} = 2\overline{)1.0}^{\,0.5} = 0.5$

Solution A. Divide the numerator 1 by the denominator 2. To make this possible, add a decimal point and a 0 after the 1, giving 10 tenths; that is, 1.0. Dividing by 2 now gives 5 tenths or 0.5.

Example B $\quad \dfrac{3}{125} = 125\overline{)3.000}^{\,0.024} = 0.024$

Solution B. Add a decimal point and two 0's after the 3, making 300 hundredths; that is, 3.00. Now divide by 125, giving 2 hundredths or 0.02. As there is a remainder, supply additional 0's and continue the division.

Example C $\quad 0.0325 = \dfrac{325}{10{,}000} = \dfrac{13}{400}$

Solution C. For the numerator of the result, write the decimal as a whole number. For the denominator, write 1, followed by as many 0's as there are places in the original decimal. Change to lowest terms.

BASIC TIME — 13 Minutes *(Estimated time to obtain a basic score of 100)*

Change to common fractions in lowest terms. Place each answer in the appropriate space on the right. (8 each)

1. 0.15 =
2. 0.04 =
3. 0.025 =
4. 0.012 =
5. 0.375 =
6. 0.0001 =
7. 0.01275 =
8. 0.1272 =
9. 0.00025 =
10. 0.02075 =
11. 0.6336 =
12. 0.5478 =

Change to equivalent decimal fractions. Round at the sixth decimal place where applicable. (8 each)

13. $\dfrac{3}{8} =$
14. $\dfrac{7}{16} =$
15. $\dfrac{24}{25} =$
16. $\dfrac{25}{32} =$
17. $\dfrac{5}{64} =$
18. $\dfrac{49}{125} =$
19. $\dfrac{2}{128} =$
20. $\dfrac{3}{250} =$
21. $\dfrac{1}{500} =$
22. $\dfrac{5}{7} =$
23. $\dfrac{13}{15} =$
24. $\dfrac{1}{124} =$
25. $\dfrac{3}{440} =$

Test 54

Name _____ Total Score _____

Date _____ Basic Score __100__

Basic Time — 9 Minutes Improvement Score _____

Change to common fractions in lowest terms. Place each answer in the appropriate space on the right. (8 each)

1. $0.25 =$
2. $0.05 =$
3. $0.125 =$
4. $0.005 =$
5. $0.025 =$
6. $0.0005 =$
7. $0.0125 =$
8. $0.625 =$
9. $0.0025 =$
10. $0.00125 =$
11. $0.3125 =$
12. $0.0375 =$

1. _____
2. _____
3. _____
4. _____
5. _____
6. _____
7. _____
8. _____
9. _____
10. _____
11. _____
12. _____

Change to equivalent decimal fractions. Round at the sixth decimal place where applicable. Place each answer in the appropriate space on the right. (8 each)

13. $\dfrac{5}{8} =$
14. $\dfrac{3}{16} =$
15. $\dfrac{9}{10} =$
16. $\dfrac{13}{25} =$
17. $\dfrac{15}{32} =$
18. $\dfrac{27}{125} =$
19. $\dfrac{13}{128} =$
20. $\dfrac{3}{1000} =$
21. $\dfrac{16}{50} =$
22. $\dfrac{2}{3} =$
23. $\dfrac{15}{16} =$
24. $\dfrac{8}{27} =$
25. $\dfrac{17}{45} =$

13. _____
14. _____
15. _____
16. _____
17. _____
18. _____
19. _____
20. _____
21. _____
22. _____
23. _____
24. _____
25. _____

Exercise 55: Decimal Equivalents

BASIC TIME — 7 Minutes *(Estimated time to obtain a basic score of 100)*

Supply decimal fractions for the fifty common fractions listed below. Show the decimal fractions as hundredths. (4 each)

NO.	COMMON FRACTION	DECIMAL FRACTION	NO.	COMMON FRACTION	DECIMAL FRACTION
1.	$\frac{1}{3}$		26.	$\frac{8}{9}$	
2.	$\frac{2}{3}$		27.	$\frac{1}{10}$	
3.	$\frac{1}{4}$		28.	$\frac{3}{10}$	
4.	$\frac{3}{4}$		29.	$\frac{7}{10}$	
5.	$\frac{1}{5}$		30.	$\frac{9}{10}$	
6.	$\frac{2}{5}$		31.	$\frac{1}{11}$	
7.	$\frac{3}{5}$		32.	$\frac{2}{11}$	
8.	$\frac{4}{5}$		33.	$\frac{1}{12}$	
9.	$\frac{1}{6}$		34.	$\frac{5}{12}$	
10.	$\frac{5}{6}$		35.	$\frac{7}{12}$	
11.	$\frac{1}{7}$		36.	$\frac{11}{12}$	
12.	$\frac{2}{7}$		37.	$\frac{1}{13}$	
13.	$\frac{3}{7}$		38.	$\frac{1}{14}$	
14.	$\frac{4}{7}$		39.	$\frac{1}{15}$	
15.	$\frac{5}{7}$		40.	$\frac{2}{15}$	
16.	$\frac{6}{7}$		41.	$\frac{1}{16}$	
17.	$\frac{1}{8}$		42.	$\frac{3}{16}$	
18.	$\frac{3}{8}$		43.	$\frac{5}{16}$	
19.	$\frac{5}{8}$		44.	$\frac{7}{16}$	
20.	$\frac{7}{8}$		45.	$\frac{11}{16}$	
21.	$\frac{1}{9}$		46.	$\frac{13}{16}$	
22.	$\frac{2}{9}$		47.	$\frac{15}{16}$	
23.	$\frac{4}{9}$		48.	$\frac{1}{20}$	
24.	$\frac{5}{9}$		49.	$\frac{1}{25}$	
25.	$\frac{7}{9}$		50.	$\frac{1}{40}$	

Test 55

Name: _____ Total Score: _____
Date: _____ Basic Score: __100__
Basic Time — 8 Minutes   Improvement Score: _____

Fill in all spaces with the equivalents called for in the column headings. Show the common fractions in lowest terms and the decimal fractions as hundredths. (4 each)

NO.	COMMON FRACTION	DECIMAL FRACTION	NO.	COMMON FRACTION	DECIMAL FRACTION
1.		1.50	26.		$0.12\frac{1}{2}$
2.		$0.02\frac{1}{2}$	27.	$\frac{7}{20}$	
3.	$\frac{1}{50}$		28.	$\frac{4}{7}$	
4.	$1\frac{1}{4}$		29.		$0.14\frac{2}{7}$
5.		$0.07\frac{1}{2}$	30.	$\frac{1}{800}$	
6.	$\frac{3}{20}$		31.		$0.83\frac{1}{3}$
7.		0.05	32.		0.80
8.		$0.93\frac{3}{4}$	33.	$\frac{9}{20}$	
9.	$\frac{1}{100}$		34.	$\frac{6}{10}$	
10.	$\frac{5}{80}$		35.		1.20
11.		$0.13\frac{1}{3}$	36.	$1\frac{1}{6}$	
12.	$2\frac{1}{5}$		37.		0.73
13.		$0.08\frac{1}{3}$	38.		0.25
14.		$0.09\frac{1}{11}$	39.	$1\frac{7}{8}$	
15.	$\frac{5}{20}$		40.	$\frac{97}{100}$	
16.	$\frac{9}{10}$		41.		$0.66\frac{2}{3}$
17.		0.70	42.	$1\frac{7}{10}$	
18.	$\frac{2}{25}$		43.		1.90
19.		$0.88\frac{8}{9}$	44.		3.50
20.		$0.11\frac{1}{9}$	45.	$2\frac{3}{4}$	
21.	$\frac{1}{200}$		46.	$10\frac{1}{2}$	
22.	$\frac{7}{8}$		47.		$0.33\frac{1}{3}$
23.		$0.62\frac{1}{2}$	48.	$1\frac{3}{5}$	
24.	$\frac{3}{50}$		49.		1.05
25.		$0.37\frac{1}{2}$	50.	$\frac{5}{6}$	

Exercise 56 — Placement of the Decimal Point

Since the proper placement of the decimal point seems to cause trouble, its placement in addition, subtraction, and multiplication is considered in this exercise. Division of decimals is discussed in Exercise 59.

When adding and subtracting decimals, align the decimal points, thus keeping each digit in its own column. See the addition problem in Example A. Add zeros in the minuend for subtraction, if desired.

When multiplying decimals, multiply them as whole numbers. Then mark off in the product the same number of decimal places as found in both the multiplier and multiplicand. See Example B.

Example A Add 3.14 + 18.4 + 340.1:

```
   3.14
  18.4
 340.1
 ─────
 361.64
```

Example B Multiply 40.8 × 3.02:

```
    40.8   1 decimal place
   ×3.02   2 decimal places
   ─────
     816
  122 40
  ──────
  123.216  3 decimal places
```

BASIC TIME — 10 Minutes *(Estimated time to obtain a basic score of 100)*

Add:

1. 325.025
    16.05
    0.3684
    1.5
    25.0725
    6.1728
    143.375   (10)

2. 3.6024 + 18.32 + 51.05 + 16.5 + 187.16 + 0.0275 = _____ (24)

3. 187.1 + 0.09275 + 3.875 + 0.005 + 18.75 + 62.0045 = _____ (24)

4. 0.02768 + 5.125 + 1376.0048 + 62.476 + 3.2 + 5.84 = _____ (24)

5. 90 + 0.028 + 3.005 + 76 + 0.02 + 15.8 + 1.1652 = _____ (24)

Subtract:

6. 18.3476
    8.09   (4)

7. 25.025
    0.97875   (4)

8. 38.1 − 4.56789 = _____ (6)

9. 257 − 152.0672 = _____ (6)

10. 0.0947 − 0.00965 = _____ (6)

11. 13.4786 − 2.75 = _____ (6)

12. 4.92 − 3.8769 = _____ (6)

13. 125 − 27.00912 = _____ (6)

14. 0.57 − 0.001027 = _____ (6)

Multiply:

15. 16.535
     385.02   (16)

16. 25.376
     4.27   (14)

17. 14.267
     0.0095   (14)

Test 56

Name _____ **Total Score** _____
Date _____ **Basic Score** 100
Basic Time — 10 Minutes **Improvement Score** _____

Add:

1. $324.3025 + 0.02 + 34.786 + 1.00055 + 0.375 + 6.248 + 16.01 + 0.025 + 14.25 =$ _____ (28)

2. $17.2 + 185 + 0.0384 + 6 + 8.478 + 0.025 =$ _____ (20)

3. $0.0274 + 3.8 + 165 + 24.5675 + 0.0027 =$ _____ (20)

4. $6.2784 + 0.02 + 3.875 + 14.1 + 16.01 + 5.5 =$ _____ (20)

5. $2.005 + 0.0375 + 14.1875 + 7.75 + 0.025 =$ _____ (20)

Subtract: (4 each)

6. $13.025 - 0.9875 =$ _____
7. $6.76 - 4.9125 =$ _____
8. $54.1 - 1.8257 =$ _____
9. $7.548 - 0.9786 =$ _____
10. $725 - 0.0937 =$ _____
11. $81.24 - 0.9876 =$ _____
12. $4.21 - 2.987 =$ _____
13. $6,421 - 0.0247 =$ _____

Multiply: (10 each)

14.   0.00487
     × 0.00421

15.   3.875
     × 0.008

16.   56.021
     × 0.0078

17.   0.6529
     × 0.426

18.   0.000271
     × 0.424

19.   72.412
     × 725

Exercise 57: Figuring a Payroll

One practical use of your knowledge of multiplication is in figuring your earnings. In business, such knowledge is used in the preparation of a payroll.

In this exercise, add each horizontal row of figures under "Hrs. Worked Daily" and place the sum on the line under "Total Hrs. Week." Then multiply the wages per hour by the total number of hours worked by each employee. Enter the results in the column headed "Gross Wages." Then total this column.

BASIC TIME — 7 Minutes *(Estimated time to obtain a basic score of 100)*

Complete the following payroll: (4 each, Total Hrs. Week column; 12 each, Gross Wages column; 8, Total)

PAYROLL   Date _____

EMPLOYEE	M	T	W	T	F	S	TOTAL HRS. WEEK	WAGES PER HR.	GROSS WAGES
Chrisman, W.	8	8	8	8	8	0		8 55	
Donosky, J.	8	8	6	8	8	0		5 90	
Fernandez, P.	8	8	8	8	8	0		7 10	
Glover, J.	0	8	8	8	8	0		8 25	
Helm, G. G.	8	8	7	8	8	0		5 50	
Hillman, E. P.	8	7	6	8	8	0		6 10	
Juarez, E.	8	8	8	8	8	0		5 97	
Klein, A. A.	8	7	5	8	8	0		8 95	
Liang, C.	8	8	5	8	8	0		6 05	
Peek, K.	8	8	8	8	7	0		7 50	
Pritchard, M.	8	8	4	0	8	0		6 40	
Towers, H.	8	8	4	8	8	0		5 80	
								Total	

Test 57

Name _____ **Total Score** _____

Date _____ **Basic Score** 100

Basic Time — 14 Minutes **Improvement Score** _____

Complete the following payroll: (4 each, Total Hrs. Week column; 12 each, Gross Wages column; 8, Total)

PAYROLL   Date _____

EMPLOYEE	M	T	W	T	F	S	TOTAL HRS. WEEK	WAGES PER HR.	GROSS WAGES
Aiken, D.	8	8	8	8	8	0		8 10	
Bernstein, L.	8	8	8	4	8	0		5 10	
Campbell, J.	0	4	8	8	8	0		6 25	
Chancey, W.	8	8	8	8	8	0		9 05	
Crisp, M.	8	8	8	8	8	0		6 50	
Griffiths, M.	8	8	8	5	8	0		7 97	
Guerra, M.	8	8	8	8	7	0		5 97	
Horn, A.B.	8	4	8	8	8	0		8 85	
Ing, C.	4	8	8	8	7	0		6 95	
Jensen, J.	8	8	8	6	8	0		7 05	
Klem, M.S.	8	8	7	7	8	0		5 40	
Laredo, C.	8	8	8	8	5	0		9 30	
Malkovich, D.	5	8	8	8	8	0		6 20	
Newsome, C.	8	8	6	8	8	0		5 25	
Orson, W.A.	8	8	8	4	8	0		7 15	
Ponsette, J.	8	8	8	8	8	0		6 75	
Powell, E.	8	8	8	8	8	0		8 52	
Ryan, C.	8	2	8	8	8	0		5 10	
Steinberg, B.	8	8	8	8	1	0		6 75	
Thomas, R.	8	8	8	8	7	0		7 99	
Uttman, G.	8	7	7	7	7	0		5 99	
Vergari, D.	8	8	8	8	4	0		9 15	
Walken, G.	8	8	8	8	8	0		6 85	
Young, V.C.	8	8	3	8	8	0		7 20	
								Total	

Exercise 58 Piecework Payroll

In some manufacturing industries, workers are paid on the basis of the number of pieces of work they do. In this exercise, you are asked to complete a piecework payroll. First, add horizontally to find the number of pieces of work completed during the week by each employee. Then, to find the wages due, multiply the number of pieces by the rate per piece. Enter this amount in the column at the right.

You will observe that the heading for this right-hand column is "Gross Pay." This term means the amount of money earned before any tax or other deductions are made by the employer to meet the government's requirements for income taxes to be withheld from the employee, and also for social security payments to be made by the employee. Such amounts are deductions from "Gross Pay," and the result is the *net*, or *take-home*, pay.

BASIC TIME — 12 Minutes *(Estimated time to obtain a basic score of 100)*

Complete the payroll below: (5 each, Total Pieces column; 10 each, Gross Pay column; 20, Total)

PAYROLL Date _____

EMPLOYEE	M	T	W	T	F	S	TOTAL PIECES	RATE	GROSS PAY
Braden, E.	54	56	72	45	61	0		1 57	
Champeau, J.	45	65	55	57	59	0		1 43	
Fisher, H.	63	65	67	68	71	0		1 38	
Gordon, M.	62	64	66	67	69	0		1 64	
Moore, G.	67	67	68	69	74	0		1 35	
Norris, A.	74	77	72	74	75	0		1 40	
Okano, B.	67	68	65	61	62	0		1 48	
Perez, B.	55	56	54	50	45	0		1 71	
Ruemmler, W.	43	42	41	51	52	0		1 45	
Schaefer, L.	44	44	47	50	51	0		1 82	
Trent, J.	45	51	51	51	53	0		1 36	
Weinstein, C.	51	61	65	62	41	0		1 39	
								Total	

Test 58

Name	Total Score	
Date	Basic Score	100
Basic Time — 20 Minutes	Improvement Score	

Complete the following piecework payroll: (3 each, Total Pieces column; 6 each, Gross Pay column; 20, Total)

PAYROLL Date _____

EMPLOYEE NO.	M	T	W	T	F	S	TOTAL PIECES	RATE	GROSS PAY
1011	55	52	53	54	55	0		1 85	
1012	56	61	57	58	59	0		1 97	
1013	57	58	59	60	61	0		1 78	
1014	61	60	61	59	50	0		1 39	
1015	45	50	51	56	57	0		1 54	
1016	51	56	49	51	53	0		1 96	
1017	55	56	57	51	49	0		1 89	
1018	56	49	51	52	53	0		1 63	
1019	57	58	59	61	49	0		1 45	
1020	51	49	51	48	52	0		1 90	
1021	48	52	49	51	50	0		1 85	
1022	51	56	57	58	41	0		1 39	
1023	49	39	69	54	52	0		1 54	
1024	56	71	65	68	69	0		1 38	
1025	61	62	63	65	67	0		1 85	
1026	43	42	41	45	51	0		1 41	
1027	42	43	45	51	47	0		1 62	
1028	42	43	44	46	47	0		1 87	
1029	51	52	53	55	61	0		1 52	
1030	45	46	47	48	48	0		1 41	
								Total	

Exercise 59 — Division of Decimals

To divide decimals, divide as in whole numbers. But before starting the division, move the decimal point in the divisor enough places to the right to make it a whole number. Then move the decimal point in the dividend the same number of places, adding 0's if necessary. Place the decimal point for the quotient directly above the new position of the decimal point in the dividend. Then proceed to divide. The division may be continued by adding as many 0's as desired.

```
                         3.7 quotient
    divisor 2.25. ) 8.32.5 dividend
                         6 75
                         1 575
                         1 575
```

BASIC TIME — 7 Minutes *(Estimated time to obtain a basic score of 100)*

Divide. Round at the fifth decimal place where applicable. Place each answer in the appropriate space on the right. (20 each, Problems 1–4; 30 each, Problems 5–8)

1. 12.71) 185.566

2. 75.14) 147.287

3. 26.4) 1,071.84

4. 42.5) 0.00978

5. 98.75) 0.025

6. 3,275) 1.15

7. 0.567) 68.4

8. 0.0347) 78.

1. _____
2. _____
3. _____
4. _____
5. _____
6. _____
7. _____
8. _____

Test 59

Name _____ Total Score _____
Date _____ Basic Score __100__
Basic Time — 5 Minutes Improvement Score _____

Divide. Round at the fifth decimal place where applicable. Place each answer in the appropriate space on the right. (20 each)

1. $2.5 \overline{)0.0635}$ 2. $0.00025 \overline{)38.}$ 1. _____

   2. _____

   3. _____

3. $78.6 \overline{)999.006}$ 4. $387 \overline{)0.0062}$

   4. _____

   5. _____

5. $5.46 \overline{)0.001}$ 6. $0.000125 \overline{)50}$

   6. _____

   7. _____

7. $0.0625 \overline{)0.12}$ 8. $0.364 \overline{)109.2}$

   8. _____

   9. _____

9. $0.012 \overline{)1}$ 10. $0.07 \overline{)1.3265}$ 10. _____

Exercise 60 — Shortcut Division by 10 and by Multiples of 10

To divide by 10, 100, 1,000, etc., move the decimal point in the dividend to the left as many places as there are 0's in the divisor. When necessary, add 0's on the left as place holders. See Example A.

Example A

365 ÷ 10 = 36.5   point moved 1 place to left
365 ÷ 100 = 3.65   point moved 2 places to left
365 ÷ 1,000 = 0.365   point moved 3 places to left
365 ÷ 10,000 = 0.0365   point moved 4 places to left

This rule may be extended to divide rapidly by any number ending in one or more 0's, such as 40, 700, and 3,000. To divide by any number ending in one or more 0's: (1) move the decimal point in the divisor to the left the number of places necessary to eliminate its 0's; (2) move the decimal point in the dividend the same number of places to the left; (3) then proceed to divide. See Example B.

Example B

$$700 \overline{)25.90} \quad \text{or} \quad 700 \overline{).25.9}$$

quotient 0.037; 21 00; 4 900; 4 900   quotient 0.037; 21; 4 9; 4 9

When both the divisor and the dividend are divided by the same number (except 0), the value of the quotient remains unchanged. Thus, when both the divisor and the dividend in Example B are divided by 100, the size of the divisor and dividend is decreased, but the value of the quotient remains unchanged. It is easier to divide by the decreased divisor.

BASIC TIME — 8 Minutes (Estimated time to obtain a basic score of 100)

Divide. Round at the fourth decimal place where applicable. (8 each)

1. 345 ÷ 10 =
2. 376 ÷ 20 =
3. 393 ÷ 30 =
4. 367 ÷ 100 =
5. 303 ÷ 200 =
6. 382.2 ÷ 300 =
7. 350 ÷ 1,000 =
8. 483 ÷ 2,000
9. 40.5 ÷ 3,000 =
10. 4.16 ÷ 40 =
11. 492 ÷ 600 =
12. 54.4 ÷ 8,000 =
13. 0.653 ÷ 500 =
14. 56.4 ÷ 60 =
15. 6,055 ÷ 700 =
16. 607 ÷ 400 =
17. 61.3 ÷ 5,000 =
18. 7.829 ÷ 9,000 =
19. 740 ÷ 800 =
20. 0.873 ÷ 50 =
21. 80.8 ÷ 900 =
22. 9.254 ÷ 70 =
23. 90.96 ÷ 60.00 =
24. 91.30 ÷ 40.00 =
25. 119.7 ÷ 70.00 =

Test 60

Name _____ Total Score _____

Date _____ Basic Score __100__

Basic Time — 15 Minutes Improvement Score _____

Divide. Round at the fourth decimal place where applicable. (4 each)

1. $34 \div 10 =$ _____
2. $96 \div 100 =$ _____
3. $89 \div 1{,}000 =$ _____
4. $31 \div 20 =$ _____
5. $35.7 \div 900 =$ _____
6. $46 \div 200 =$ _____
7. $48 \div 3{,}000$ _____
8. $47 \div 10 =$ _____
9. $42 \div 70 =$ _____
10. $57 \div 100.00 =$ _____
11. $57 \div 40 =$ _____
12. $56 \div 100 =$ _____
13. $63 \div 3{,}000 =$ _____
14. $66.5 \div 70 =$ _____
15. $75 \div 300 =$ _____
16. $79 \div 4{,}000 =$ _____
17. $85.4 \div 80 =$ _____
18. $98 \div 5{,}000 =$ _____
19. $9.36 \div 400 =$ _____
20. $10.17 \div 90 =$ _____
21. $1.07 \div 90 =$ _____
22. $112 \div 60.00 =$ _____
23. $110 \div 800.00 =$ _____
24. $337 \div 60 =$ _____
25. $80 \div 400 =$ _____

26. $357 \div 4{,}000 =$ _____
27. $37.6 \div 20 =$ _____
28. $393 \div 600 =$ _____
29. $43.92 \div 30 =$ _____
30. $4.92 \div 80 =$ _____
31. $43.1 \div 1{,}000 =$ _____
32. $57.47 \div 7{,}000$ _____
33. $510 \div 50.00 =$ _____
34. $534 \div 30 =$ _____
35. $632 \div 800 =$ _____
36. $645 \div 500.0 =$ _____
37. $681 \div 700 =$ _____
38. $728 \div 50 =$ _____
39. $748 \div 40.00 =$ _____
40. $862 \div 20{,}000 =$ _____
41. $823.8 \div 6{,}000 =$ _____
42. $94.72 \div 800 =$ _____
43. $9.906 \div 60 =$ _____
44. $105.8 \div 500 =$ _____
45. $108.16 \div 700.00 =$ _____
46. $1.159 \div 90 =$ _____
47. $0.768 \div 80.00 =$ _____
48. $3.564 \div 600.0 =$ _____
49. $3{,}768 \div 4{,}000 =$ _____
50. $39.097 \div 9{,}000 =$ _____

Exercise 61 — Aliquot Parts

A number (whole or mixed) that divides into another number leaving no remainder is called an **aliquot part** of that number. Therefore, 5 is an aliquot part of 10, 4 is an aliquot part of 12, $12\frac{1}{2}$ is an aliquot part of 100, and 25 is an aliquot part of 100. Looking at this relationship in another way, 5 is to 10 as 1 is to 2:

$$\frac{5}{10} = \frac{1}{2}$$

The relationships of the other numbers mentioned above are:

$$\frac{4}{12} = \frac{1}{3} \qquad \frac{12\frac{1}{2}}{100} = \frac{25}{200} = \frac{1}{8} \qquad \frac{25}{100} = \frac{1}{4}$$

Such relationships between numbers may be used to simplify the solution of a problem. An advantage of aliquot-part shortcut methods is that many problems may be solved mentally. The mental solution to the example below may be deduced in this manner: 56 pounds at $1 a pound would cost $56; but if the price were only $\frac{1}{8}$ of $1 for each pound, the cost would be only $\frac{1}{8}$ as much, or $7 ($\frac{1}{8}$ of $56).

Example 56 lb. @ $12\frac{1}{2}$¢ = _____?_____

Solution: $56 \times \$0.12\frac{1}{2} = 56 \times \$\frac{1}{8} = \$7$

Notice that when the cent sign (¢) is removed, the decimal point is moved two places to the left.

BASIC TIME — 8 Minutes *(Estimated time to obtain a basic score of 100)*

Determine the aliquot part of 100 that each of the following amounts represents: (10 each)

NO.	PROBLEM	SOLUTION	NO.	PROBLEM	SOLUTION
0.	$12\frac{1}{2}$ = $\frac{1}{8}$ of 100	$\frac{12\frac{1}{2}}{100} = \frac{25}{200} = \frac{1}{8}$	9.	75 = ____ of 100	
1.	10 = ____ of 100		10.	$87\frac{1}{2}$ = ____ of 100	
2.	20 = ____ of 100		11.	$37\frac{1}{2}$ = ____ of 100	
3.	25 = ____ of 100		12.	$41\frac{2}{3}$ = ____ of 100	
4.	40 = ____ of 100		13.	$18\frac{3}{4}$ = ____ of 100	
5.	$16\frac{2}{3}$ = ____ of 100		14.	$62\frac{1}{2}$ = ____ of 100	
6.	$33\frac{1}{3}$ = ____ of 100		15.	$83\frac{1}{3}$ = ____ of 100	
7.	$8\frac{1}{3}$ = ____ of 100		16.	$14\frac{2}{7}$ = ____ of 100	
8.	$6\frac{1}{4}$ = ____ of 100		17.	$11\frac{1}{9}$ = ____ of 100	

In the parentheses show the aliquot part of $1 for each price and determine the total cost: (2 each for aliquot part; 4 each for total cost)

0. 64 @ 10¢ ($\frac{1}{10}$) = $6.40

18. 40 @ 5¢ (____) = $____

19. 84 @ 25¢ (____) = $____

20. 670 @ 50¢ (____) = $____

21. 575 @ 20¢ (____) = $____

22. 864 @ $16\frac{2}{3}$¢ (____) = $____

Test 61

Name _____ Total Score _____
Date _____ Basic Score   100
Basic Time — 10 Minutes   Improvement Score _____

Determine the aliquot part of 100 that each of the following amounts represents: (4 each)

NO.	PROBLEM	SOLUTION	NO.	PROBLEM	SOLUTION
1.	$25 = $ _____ of 100		12.	$18\frac{3}{4} = $ _____ of 100	
2.	$33\frac{1}{3} = $ _____ of 100		13.	$93\frac{3}{4} = $ _____ of 100	
3.	$75 = $ _____ of 100		14.	$66\frac{2}{3} = $ _____ of 100	
4.	$16\frac{2}{3} = $ _____ of 100		15.	$87\frac{1}{2} = $ _____ of 100	
5.	$14\frac{2}{7} = $ _____ of 100		16.	$60 = $ _____ of 100	
6.	$8\frac{1}{3} = $ _____ of 100		17.	$12\frac{1}{2} = $ _____ of 100	
7.	$6\frac{1}{4} = $ _____ of 100		18.	$11\frac{1}{9} = $ _____ of 100	
8.	$37\frac{1}{2} = $ _____ of 100		19.	$41\frac{2}{3} = $ _____ of 100	
9.	$83\frac{1}{3} = $ _____ of 100		20.	$91\frac{2}{3} = $ _____ of 100	
10.	$62\frac{1}{2} = $ _____ of 100		21.	$43\frac{3}{4} = $ _____ of 100	
11.	$58\frac{1}{3} = $ _____ of 100		22.	$56\frac{1}{4} = $ _____ of 100	

In the parentheses show each price as an aliquot part of $1 and determine the total cost: (4 each for aliquot part; 4 each for total cost)

23. 60 @ 50¢ (_____) = $ _____   30. 56 @ $14\frac{2}{7}$¢ (_____) = $ _____
24. 64 @ 25¢ (_____) = $ _____   31. 72 @ $11\frac{1}{9}$¢ (_____) = $ _____
25. 64 @ $12\frac{1}{2}$¢ (_____) = $ _____   32. 588 @ $8\frac{1}{3}$¢ (_____) = $ _____
26. 84 @ $16\frac{2}{3}$¢ (_____) = $ _____   33. 480 @ $6\frac{1}{4}$¢ (_____) = $ _____
27. 471 @ $33\frac{1}{3}$¢ (_____) = $ _____   34. 480 @ 75¢ (_____) = $ _____
28. 375 @ 20¢ (_____) = $ _____   35. 480 @ 60¢ (_____) = $ _____
29. 306 @ $16\frac{2}{3}$¢ (_____) = $ _____   36. 805 @ 80¢ (_____) = $ _____

Exercise 62 Application Problems

BASIC TIME — 10 Minutes *(Estimated time to obtain a basic score of 100)*

Solve these problems. Write each answer in the appropriate space on the right. (20 each)

1. How much will 25 pen sets cost at $7.98 each?... _____

2. An order for $16\frac{2}{3}$ dozen mechanical pencils costs $24.50. What is the cost per dozen pencils?.. _____

3. If 4 small bolts can be bought for 35¢, how many bolts can be bought for $5.25?.. _____

4. A certain steel beam weighs 18.4 pounds per foot of length. If this beam is 26.5 feet long, how many pounds does it weigh?... _____

5. The monthly salary of Julia Price increased from $1,865 to $2,953.75 over a period of 4.5 years. On the average, how much did her monthly salary increase per year? *(Round to nearest cent.)* .... _____

6. The total cost, including carrying charges, for the boat which Mr. Thomas purchased was $6,943.76. He paid $2,750 down and agreed to pay the balance in 12 equal monthly payments. How much was each payment?................................. _____

7. Last year a family paid $10,500 for doctors' bills. If this is equal to 0.30 of the family's annual income, how much was the annual income?................................ _____

8. An automobile used 541 gallons of gasoline while being driven 9,088.8 miles. (a) What was the average number of miles driven per gallon? (b) At $1.428 a gallon, what was the gasoline cost per mile? ....

   (a) _____

   (b) _____

9. Ruben Diaz set a goal to earn $400 in commissions for the week before Christmas. Commissions for each sales day of the week were: $67.14, $76.29, $50.34, $46.10, $67.30, and $79.07. How much less than the goal was earned in commissions?... _____

10. Kate and Jerry McLean paid $180 as a down payment on a refrigerator that cost $938.52 including the service charges. What is the amount of each payment if they are to pay the balance in 12 equal payments?... _____

126

Test 62

Name _____ Total Score _____

Date _____ Basic Score   __100__

Basic Time — 10 Minutes Improvement Score _____

Solve these problems. Write each answer in the appropriate space on the right. (20 each)

1. The Olsens want to insure their house for $165,000. The insurance company charges an annual premium of 33⅓¢ per $100 of insurance for this type of policy. How much is the annual premium? .... _____

2. How much will 25 dozen cookies cost at $1.39 a dozen? .... _____

3. An airplane was flown 1,298.3 miles in 3.75 hours. Find the average speed to the nearest tenth of a mile per hour. .... _____

4. Agnes McCray received commissions totaling $52.95 for having made 29 sales. To the nearest cent, what was the average amount of commission on each sale?... _____

5. A store bought 250 toys at $6.97 each to sell during the holidays. What was the total cost to the store? .... _____

6. At a cost of 57¢ a gallon, how much will it cost to fill these tanks: two main tanks with a capacity of 165 gallons each and two auxiliary tanks with a capacity of 24 gallons each? .... _____

7. John Mako earns $6.25 an hour working after class and on Saturdays. He works 4½ hours on each of five days and 8 hours on Saturday. How much is his gross weekly wages? .... _____

8. Find the total cost of 6 battery-operated toys at $17.95 each and 14 batteries at 2 for $1.59 .... _____

9. Cindy Maffey bought 10 gallons of unleaded gasoline for her car and 12 gallons of regular gasoline for her son's car. She noticed that the unleaded gasoline cost $1.369 per gallon. The total cost of the gasoline for both cars was $29.35. How much was the cost of the regular gasoline per gallon? .... _____

10. The length of the tunnel is 5.4 miles. If an automobile traveled at the speed limit of 45 miles per hour, how many minutes (*to the nearest tenth*) would it take to go through the tunnel? .... _____

Exercise 63 — Percent Equivalents

In practical mathematics, percent is often useful. **Percent** means **hundredths**. One hundred percent means one hundred one-hundredths. Five percent means five one-hundredths and may be written in three ways: $\frac{5}{100}$, 0.05, and 5%. *All have the same mathematical value.*

You should know four rules for changing these forms from one to the other. (1) To change a percent to a decimal fraction, remove the percent sign (%) and move the decimal point two places to the left (25% = 0.25 and $33\frac{1}{3}\%$ = $0.33\frac{1}{3}$). (2) To change a percent to a common fraction, first change the percent to a decimal fraction and then to a common fraction expressed in lowest terms (25% = 0.25 = $\frac{25}{100} = \frac{1}{4}$). (3) To change a decimal fraction to a percent, move the decimal point two places to the right and add a percent sign (0.2 = 20%). (4) To change a common fraction to a percent, first change the common fraction to a decimal fraction and then change the decimal fraction to a percent according to the rule in (3) above ($\frac{1}{20}$ = 0.05 = 5%).

BASIC TIME — 10 Minutes *(Estimated time to obtain a basic score of 100)*

Change each of the following percents to a decimal fraction equivalent: (4 each)

	DECIMAL FRACTION			DECIMAL FRACTION			DECIMAL FRACTION
1. 40% =	_____	4. 75% =	_____	7. $7\frac{1}{2}$% =	_____
2. 2% =	_____	5. $\frac{1}{4}$% =	_____	8. $66\frac{2}{3}$% =	_____
3. 125% =	_____	6. 7% =	_____	9. 750% =	_____

Change each of the following percents to decimal and common fraction equivalents: (4 each answer)

	DECIMAL FRACTION	COMMON FRACTION			DECIMAL FRACTION	COMMON FRACTION
10. 10% =	_____	_____	15. $\frac{3}{4}$% =	_____	_____
11. $33\frac{1}{3}$% =	_____	_____	16. 70% =	_____	_____
12. 25% =	_____	_____	17. $8\frac{1}{3}$% =	_____	_____
13. 5% =	_____	_____	18. 875% =	_____	_____
14. 135% =	_____	_____	19. $62\frac{1}{2}$% =	_____	_____

Change each of the following decimal fractions to a percent: (4 each)

	PERCENT			PERCENT			PERCENT
20. 0.45 =	_____	23. 0.80 =	_____	26. $1.37\frac{1}{2}$ =	_____
21. 0.6 =	_____	24. $0.00\frac{1}{4}$ =	_____	27. $0.00\frac{1}{5}$ =	_____
22. 2.35 =	_____	25. 0.8 =	_____	28. $0.06\frac{1}{4}$ =	_____

Change each common fraction and mixed number to a percent correct to the nearest tenth of a percent: (4 each)

	PERCENT			PERCENT			PERCENT
29. $\frac{1}{2}$ =	_____	33. $\frac{3}{8}$ =	_____	37. $4\frac{3}{4}$ =	_____
30. $\frac{1}{4}$ =	_____	34. $\frac{1}{50}$ =	_____	38. $\frac{1}{3}$ =	_____
31. $\frac{2}{5}$ =	_____	35. $2\frac{2}{3}$ =	_____	39. $\frac{7}{20}$ =	_____
32. $\frac{1}{6}$ =	_____	36. $\frac{5}{8}$ =	_____	40. $\frac{1}{160}$ =	_____

Test 63

Name _____ Total Score ____

Date _____ Basic Score __100__

Basic Time — 10 Minutes Improvement Score ____

Supply the equivalent common fractions, decimal fractions, and percents in the table below. Show the common fractions in lowest terms and the decimal fractions as hundredths. (4 each)

Use this space for computations	NO.	COMMON FRACTIONS	DECIMAL FRACTIONS	PERCENTS
	1.	$\frac{1}{2}$		
	2.		1.25	
	3.			$16\frac{2}{3}\%$
	4.	$\frac{5}{8}$		
	5.		0.10	
	6.			125%
	7.	$2\frac{3}{4}$		
	8.		$1.33\frac{1}{3}$	
	9.			$62\frac{1}{2}\%$
	10.	$\frac{7}{8}$		
	11.		4.75	
	12.			$1\frac{1}{2}\%$
	13.	$\frac{17}{50}$		
	14.		$0.00\frac{1}{4}$	
	15.			$\frac{1}{8}\%$
	16.	$\frac{2}{3}$		
	17.		0.03	
	18.			15%
	19.	$\frac{1}{8}$		
	20.		$0.62\frac{1}{2}$	
	21.			$87\frac{1}{2}\%$
	22.	$\frac{4}{5}$		
	23.		$0.00\frac{1}{2}$	
	24.			$6\frac{1}{4}\%$
	25.	$1\frac{1}{10}$		

Exercise 64 Percentage Problems

The three basic problems in percentage are illustrated below.

1. To find the amount that is a certain percent of a given number, multiply the number given by the percent.

   Example A What number is 4% of 600?
   Solution: 600 × 0.04 = 24.00

2. To find the percent one number is of another, divide the number by that other number.

Example B 30 is what percent of 500?
Solution: 30 ÷ 500 = 0.06 = 6%

3. To find the base number when an amount and a percent are given, divide the amount given by the percent.

Example C 40 is 5% of what number?
Solution: 40 ÷ 0.05 = 800

BASIC TIME — 16 Minutes *(Estimated time to obtain a basic score of 100)*

Solve these problems. Write the answers in the spaces on the right. (10 each)

1. How much is 25% of 384? ....
2. What number is 225% of 328? ....
3. What percent of 360 is 45? ....
4. What percent of 460 is 690? ....
5. The number 62 is 5% of what number? ....
6. The number 63 is 35% of what number? ....
7. What number is 9% of 5? ....
8. The number 42 is what percent of 48? ....
9. The number 836 is what percent of 1,000? ....
10. 32% of what number is 672? ....
11. 34% of what number is 306? ....
12. Find 72% of 307. ....
13. Find 432% of 106. ....
14. 95 is what percent of 47.5? ....
15. What percent of 35 is 7? ....
16. How much is $\frac{1}{2}$% of 9,815? ....
17. 70 is 215% of what number? ....
18. What number is 0.05% of 971? ....
19. What percent of 240 is 720? ....
20. 48 is what percent of 288? ....

Test 64

Name _____ Total Score _____

Date _____ Basic Score __100__

Basic Time — 18 Minutes Improvement Score _____

Solve these problems. Write the answers in the spaces on the right. (10 each)

1. What number is 21% of 6? .... _____

2. How much is 2.4% of 243? .... _____

3. What percent of 888 is 4.44? .... _____

4. What percent of 371 is 927.5? .... _____

5. The number 107.8 is 28% of what number? .... _____

6. The number 175 is 7% of what number? .... _____

7. What number is 21% of 87? .... _____

8. The number 36 is what percent of 48? .... _____

9. The number 572 is what percent of 2,000? .... _____

10. 35% of what number is 542.85? .... _____

11. 57% of what number is 1,218.66? .... _____

12. Find 126% of 89. .... _____

13. Find 48% of 564. .... _____

14. 95 is what percent of 475? .... _____

15. What percent of 45 is 135? .... _____

16. How much is $\frac{1}{4}$% of 5,476? .... _____

17. 96 is 75% of what number? .... _____

18. A merchant's sales this year are 15% greater than last year. If sales last year were $324,756.80, what are the sales this year? .... _____

19. A gain on sales of $25,624 was $8,247. The gain is what percent of sales? .... _____

20. A merchant had a gain of 25% in sales. The gain was $36,428. Find the sales. ...... _____

Exercise 65 — Commission on Sales

When goods are sold on **commission**, the amount for which the agent sells the goods to the customer is the base upon which the commission is calculated.

1. To find the amount of the commission, multiply the amount of the sales by the rate (changing the rate to a decimal fraction), as shown in Example A.
2. To find the net proceeds for the company, deduct the commission and all other charges from the sales, as shown in Example B.

Example A

Sales × Rate = Commission

$110 × 0.04 = $4.40

Example B

Sales − {Commission + Trucking + Storage + Freight} = Net Proceeds

$110 − ($4.40 + $5 + $4 + $9) = $87.60

BASIC TIME — 15 Minutes *(Estimated time to obtain a basic score of 100)*

Find the commission and the net proceeds:

#	SALES	RATE	COMMISSION	TRUCKING	STORAGE	FREIGHT	NET PROCEEDS	
1.	111.15	4%						(6)
2.	275.00	6%						(6)
3.	612.50	7½%						(8)
4.	437.25	5%						(6)
5.	368.10	6%						(6)
6.	972.38	10%				5.23		(8)
7.	517.14	6⅖%			3.75			(12)
8.	249.35	4%		2.50				(10)
9.	1,028.60	5%			4.50			(10)
10.	4,250.75	6%				9.38		(10)
11.	765.50	7%		3.75		8.63		(10)
12.	463.75	6%		2.50		7.35		(10)
13.	948.20	4%			5.00	3.78		(10)
14.	828.00	4½%		4.50	4.75			(12)
15.	367.40	5%			9.60	9.80		(10)
16.	1,941.12	5%		13.50	12.50	20.25		(12)
17.	534.28	6%		2.75	9.75	6.75		(12)
18.	4,250.00	4%		14.25	12.85	19.50		(10)
19.	638.90	7%		2.50	1.10	3.47		(10)
20.	4,571.50	6%		17.00	14.60	11.75		(10)

21. An agent sold a shipment of oranges for $1,847.25. The charges were as follows: $6 for storage, $8.75 for delivery, and 7½% commission for selling. Find the net proceeds........................ _____ (12)

Test 65

Name _____ **Total Score** _____

Date _____ **Basic Score** ____100____

Basic Time — 12 Minutes **Improvement Score** _____

Find the commission and the net proceeds:

	SALES	RATE	COMMISSION	TRUCKING	STORAGE	FREIGHT	NET PROCEEDS	
1.	2,375.00	6%		11.25				(12)
2.	1,130.50	5%						(10)
3.	713.25	7%		2.75	3.00	4.63		(14)
4.	347.60	4%		10.75		9.40		(14)
5.	481.85	6%		9.50		2.35		(14)
6.	817.15	5%		3.00	2.50	4.25		(14)
7.	623.50	4%		2.35	9.85	4.00		(14)
8.	1,250.00	6%		15.00		14.82		(12)
9.	913.75	7½%		8.50		6.38		(20)
10.	237.12	7%		9.25		2.56		(14)

11. An agent sold 1,250 bushels of a commodity at $1.88 a bushel, paid 5¢ a bushel for trucking, $78.75 for freight, kept 6% for a commission, and sent the employer a check for the net proceeds. What was the amount of the check? .... _____(24)

12. An agent sold 150 cases of canned goods, 24 cans to the case, at 39¢ a can. The shipping charges were $62.50, and the commission was 5% of sales. Find the net proceeds. .... _____(20)

13. Find the net proceeds from the sale of 124 tons at $81.75 a ton on a commission of 4½%. The other charges were $52.75. .... _____(18)

Exercise 66: Commission on Purchases

When goods are bought on commission, the amount for which the goods are bought, or the **prime cost**, is the base upon which the commission is calculated.

1. To find the amount of commission, multiply the prime cost by the rate, as shown in Example A.
2. To find the gross or total cost, add the amount of the commission and all the other charges to the prime cost, as shown in Example B.

Example A

Prime Cost × Rate = Commission

$500 × 0.05 = $25

Example B

Prime Cost + (Commission + Trucking + Storage + Freight) = Gross Cost

$500 + ($25 + $13 + $3.50 + $12) = $553.50

BASIC TIME — 15 Minutes *(Estimated time to obtain a basic score of 100)*

Find the commission and the gross cost:

#	PRIME COST	RATE	COMMISSION	TRUCKING	STORAGE	FREIGHT	GROSS COST	
1.	590.80	6%						(8)
2.	575.00	5%						(6)
3.	817.25	7%						(8)
4.	1,175.00	3½%						(8)
5.	243.20	4%						(8)
6.	1,216.75	4%		13.75				(10)
7.	912.65	6%		11.50				(10)
8.	675.00	7½%				11.42		(10)
9.	91.30	5%			5.69			(8)
10.	2,450.00	6%				32.50		(8)
11.	485.75	5%		2.75		8.43		(10)
12.	421.60	7%		9.50	2.25			(10)
13.	530.70	4%			3.50	6.88		(10)
14.	1,061.50	6%		15.50		19.32		(10)
15.	648.35	7%		12.50		7.35		(10)
16.	1,017.80	4%		13.50	17.50	16.10		(10)
17.	623.50	8%		13.00	2.50	5.76		(10)
18.	893.25	6%		4.80	2.25	5.13		(10)
19.	764.38	5%		5.50	3.75	4.38		(10)
20.	1,275.00	6%		15.75	14.50	11.23		(10)

21. An agent shipped an employer 75 bales, averaging 294 pounds each. The bales were bought at 7½¢ a pound on a commission of 6½%. The other charges were $21.75. Find the gross cost. .... _____ (16)

Test 66

Name _____ Total Score _____
Date _____   Basic Score 100
Basic Time — 10 Minutes   Improvement Score _____

Find the commission and the gross cost:

	PRIME COST	RATE	COMMISSION	TRUCKING	STORAGE	FREIGHT	GROSS COST	
1.	2,350.00	4%						(8)
2.	1,875.00	5%		13.75	9.60	12.57		(14)
3.	436.75	7%		12.50				(12)
4.	712.50	6%		5.00	13.75	4.85		(14)
5.	256.80	5%		9.25		10.88		(12)
6.	841.60	4%		10.00				(12)
7.	628.30	6%		4.25	7.00			(12)
8.	325.40	8%		2.50		9.15		(12)
9.	278.65	6%		3.75		2.16		(12)
10.	1,931.20	7%		17.75	10.00	17.13		(14)

11. An agent bought 1,125 cartons of a commodity at 70¢ a carton, paid $3\frac{1}{2}$¢ a carton for trucking and $19.50 for freight, and charged a commission of 5% for buying. What was the gross cost? .... _____ (22)

12. An agent bought 144 boxes of fruit at $6.10 a box on a commission of 6%. Other charges amounted to $9.75. Find the gross cost. .... _____ (22)

13. An agent bought 200 boxes of fruit at $4.85 a box and sold them at $5.75 a box. The commissions charged were 3% for buying and 4% for selling. The cost of handling was $12.75. Find the employer's gain. .... _____ (34)

Exercise 67 — Trade Discounts

A **trade discount** is a deduction from a catalog or a list price. When two or more trade discounts are given on one invoice, they may be referred to as a *chain* or *series of discounts*. Discounts may be computed in the order given, with the first rate based on the list price; the second, on the remainder after the amount of the first discount is deducted from the list price; and the third, on the remainder after the amount of the second discount has been subtracted.

Example A Find the net price for merchandise listed at $500, less trade discounts of 20%, 10%, and 5%:

$500 list price
 100 less first discount (20%)
$400 remainder
  40 less second discount (10%)
$360 remainder
  18 less third discount (5%)
$342 net price

To find a discount rate that is equal to a series of discounts, consider the total amount of any invoice to be equal to 100% and subtract the discount percents in the normal manner. The remainder, the **net-price percent**, subtracted from 100% gives the **equivalent discount rate**.

Example B Find the discount rate that is equal to the series of discounts 20%, 10%, and 5%:

100.0% list price percent
 20.0% less first discount (20%)
 80.0% remainder
  8.0% less second discount (10%)
 72.0% remainder
  3.6% less third discount (5%)
 68.4% net price percent

100% − 68.4% = 31.6% equivalent discount rate

BASIC TIME — 20 Minutes (Estimated time to obtain a basic score of 100)

Find the amount of discount and the net price for each of these: (8 each)

	LIST PRICE	TRADE DISCOUNTS	AMOUNT OF DISCOUNT	NET PRICE
1.	$600.00	20%, 10%		
2.	800.00	25%, 10%		
3.	480.00	30%, 25%		
4.	750.00	20%, 20%, 10%		
5.	979.47	40%, 10%, 10%		

Find the equivalent discount rate for each series of discounts: (6 each)

	SERIES OF DISCOUNTS	EQUIVALENT DISCOUNT RATE			SERIES OF DISCOUNTS	EQUIVALENT DISCOUNT RATE
6.	20%, 10%			11.	10%, 10%, 5%	
7.	25%, 10%			12.	20%, 10%, 5%	
8.	30%, 25%			13.	20%, 20%, 10%	
9.	15%, 10%			14.	40%, 10%, 10%	
10.	50%, 50%			15.	30%, 20%, 10%	

Complete this table: (4 each answer)

	LIST PRICE	TRADE DISCOUNTS	EQUIVALENT DISCOUNT RATE	AMOUNT OF DISCOUNT	NET PRICE
16.	$1,200.00	25%, 20%			
17.	2,610.00	40%, 10%			
18.	1,672.00	25%, 10%, 5%			
19.	944.80	20%, 30%, 40%			
20.	1,863.40	50%, 25%, 25%			

Test 67

Name _____ Total Score _____

Date _____ Basic Score __100__

Basic Time — 10 Minutes Improvement Score _____

Solve these problems. Write the answers in the spaces on the right. (20 each)

1. A catalog lists tires at $96 each. A discount sheet sent later to the customers of this company announces a trade discount of $18\frac{3}{4}$% on these tires. Determine the net price a customer would pay for each tire ordered. .... _____

2. An invoice totaling $2,157.30 for tools received from a tool company showed trade discounts of 20% and 10%. Determine the net price to this buyer. .... _____

3. Terra Manufacturing Company allows trade discounts of $14\frac{2}{7}$% and $12\frac{1}{2}$% to retailers. What is the net price a retailer should pay for an invoice totaling $434? ..... _____

4. A used car priced at $1,925 was sold at a 15% discount in a state that has a 4% sales tax. How much did the buyer pay for the car? .... _____

5. Westgate Company allows discounts of 25% and 10%. A company salesperson sold merchandise totaling $772 and, in error, gave an equivalent discount of 35%. How much was the salesperson's error? .... _____

6. How much should a retailer pay the manufacturer for 60 blouses listed at $45 each if trade discounts of 25% and 20% are allowed? .... _____

7. What are the equivalent discount rates for (a) discounts of 25%, 20%, and 10% and (b) discounts of 15%, 10%, and 5%? ....

    (a) _____
    (b) _____

8. Valley Camera Company's catalog lists Model B55 at $120. (a) What is the equivalent discount to Olympic Camera Shop if it is allowed discounts of $33\frac{1}{3}$% and 20%? (b) What is the net price to the shop for camera Model B55? ....

    (a) _____
    (b) _____

9. A customer saved $70 by buying a lawn mower at a sale. If the dealer allowed a discount of 25% on this model, what was the original price of the lawn mower? ..... _____

10. Which is the better buy for the customer: (a) a desk listed at $260 with discounts of 25% and 15% or (b) an equal quality desk listed at $250 with discounts of 20%, 15%, and 5%? How much better? .... _____

Exercise 68: Determining Due Dates

The **due date** for an invoice or loan is the date on which payment is due. When the time is expressed in days, the due date is exactly that number of days after the date of the loan. When the time is expressed as a number of months or years, the due date falls on the same date in the appropriate number of subsequent months or years. If the month does not contain that date, the last day of the month is taken. That is, a one-month note dated May 31 falls due on June 30. When time is given in days, there are two methods for determining due dates.

The **exact-time method** requires that you know the exact number of days in each month and whether February falls in a leap year. February in a leap year (any year date divisible by 4) has 29 days.

Example A Use the exact-time method to find the number of days from December 18, 1985, to March 14, 1987.

Dec. 18, 1985, to Dec. 18, 1986	365
Dec. 18, 1986, to Dec. 31, 1986	13
January, 1987	31
February, 1987	28
To March 14, 1987	14
Total	451 days

A leap year contains 366 days; a regular year, 365 days. See Example A for this calculation.

The **compound method** of finding the number of days between two dates is based on the business assumption that each year is composed of 12 months of 30 days each for a total of 360 days. This method involves the subtraction of the years, months, and days. Like units are arranged in columns, with the earlier date placed below the later date. As in the subtraction of any numbers, it may be necessary to "borrow" a unit from the left. See Example B.

Example B Use the compound method to find the number of days from December 18, 1985, to March 14, 1987.

Year	Month	Day
	14	
6	*2*	*44*
1987	3	14
1985	12	18
1 yr.	2 mo.	26 days

360 days + 60 days + 26 days = 446 days

BASIC TIME — 12 Minutes *(Estimated time to obtain a basic score of 100)*

Find the number of days between the dates shown using (a) the exact-time method and (b) the compound method: (10 each answer)

NUMBER OF DAYS BETWEEN DATES

	a Exact-Time Method	b Compound Method
1. January 15, 1986, to December 1, 1986	_____	_____
2. February 12, 1986, to January 16, 1987	_____	_____
3. November 3, 1986, to May 30, 1987	_____	_____
4. June 2, 1987, to May 6, 1988	_____	_____
5. November 6, 1986, to March 5, 1987	_____	_____
6. December 8, 1987, to July 20, 1988	_____	_____
7. October 1, 1990, to April 4, 1991	_____	_____

Find the due date for each of the following: (10 each)

DATE OF NOTE	TIME	DUE DATE
8. March 17, 1987	30 days	_____
9. February 26, 1986	60 days	_____
10. August 30, 1985	120 days	_____
11. July 8, 1986	3 months	_____
12. September 3, 1987	6 months	_____
13. January 25, 1989	2 years	_____

Test 68

Name _____
Date _____
Basic Time — 15 Minutes

Total Score _____
Basic Score __100__
Improvement Score _____

Find the number of days between the dates shown using (a) the exact-time method and (b) the compound method: (8 each, Column a; 6 each, Column b)

	NUMBER OF DAYS BETWEEN DATES	
	a Exact-Time Method	b Compound Method
1. February 25, 1987, to October 5, 1987	_____	_____
2. March 28, 1987, to March 1, 1988	_____	_____
3. May 14, 1989, to October 25, 1989	_____	_____
4. July 6, 1987, to January 30, 1988	_____	_____
5. September 9, 1986, to October 1, 1988	_____	_____
6. August 29, 1986, to April 1, 1987	_____	_____
7. January 16, 1988, to May 4, 1988	_____	_____
8. February 9, 1987, to January 1, 1988	_____	_____
9. April 15, 1986, to February 18, 1987	_____	_____
10. June 30, 1991, to December 4, 1991	_____	_____

Find the due date for each of the following: (6 each)

DATE OF INVOICE OR NOTE	TIME	DUE DATE
11. April 7, 1985	30 days	_____
12. February 5, 1988	45 days	_____
13. January 13, 1986	90 days	_____
14. September 24, 1987	150 days	_____
15. December 26, 1989	240 days	_____
16. March 31, 1992	3 months	_____
17. October 21, 1990	6 months	_____
18. April 30, 1989	9 months	_____
19. November 19, 1989	1½ years	_____
20. May 18, 1991	2¼ years	_____

Exercise 69 — Cash Discounts

As a means of encouraging their customers to make prompt and early payment, sellers often grant special discounts in addition to trade discounts. Such discounts granted for early payment are called **cash discounts**. They are part of the credit terms and appear on the invoice.

For example, terms of *2/10, n/30* (2% discount in 10 days, net in 30) mean the credit period is 30 days, but the buyer may deduct 2% if the invoice is paid within 10 days from date of invoice. If the invoice is not paid in 30 days, it is past due and may be subject to an interest charge or late fee. Due dates for cash discounts are calculated by the exact-time method shown in Exercise 68.

Example

What amount is needed to pay a $200 invoice, terms 2/10, n/30, if it is paid (a) within 10 days from date of invoice or (b) within 11 to 30 days from date of invoice?

(a) $200 amount after trade discounts
    4 less cash discount of 2%
    $196 amount to be paid

(b) The cash discount period has expired. Therefore, $200 (the amount of the invoice) is to be paid.

BASIC TIME — 12 Minutes (Estimated time to obtain a basic score of 100)

Find the cash discount that should be taken and the net amount for each of the following: (6 each, Cash Discount column; 4 each, Net Amount column)

	AMOUNT OF INVOICE	TERMS	CASH DISCOUNT	NET AMOUNT
1.	$760.00	2/10, n/30	15.20	744.80
2.	480.00	1/15, n/60	4.80	475.20
3.	807.00	3/20, n/60	24.21	782.79
4.	1,259.00	1/10, n/30	12.59	1,246.41
5.	3,490.00	3/30, n/90	104.70	3,385.30
6.	546.50	4/10, 2/20, n/60	21.86	524.64
7.	1,040.65	5/10, 2/30, n/60	52.03	988.62
8.	3,170.75	2/10, 1/20, n/30	63.42	3,107.33
9.	973.51	6/10, 4/30, n/90	58.41	915.10
10.	824.69	5/15, 2/30, n/60	41.23	783.46

	DATE OF INVOICE	AMOUNT OF INVOICE	TERMS	DATE PAID	CASH DISCOUNT	NET AMOUNT
11.	Mar. 13	$980.00	2/10, n/30	Mar. 22	19.60	960.40
12.	Mar. 15	660.00	3/10, 2/30, n/60	Mar. 24	19.80	640.20
13.	Mar. 18	775.80	2/10, 1/30, n/60	Apr. 11	7.76	768.04
14.	Apr. 18	1,197.00	4/10, 2/30, n/60	Apr. 28	47.88	1,149.12
15.	June 28	1,937.50	5/15, 2/30, n/60	July 13	96.88	1,840.62
16.	July 27	3,557.95	6/10, 2/40, n/90	Aug. 6	213.48	3,344.47
17.	Aug. 10	3,680.75	7/15, 4/45, n/90	Sept. 24	147.23	3,533.52
18.	Sept. 23	1,019.86	2/10, 1/20, n/60	Oct. 14	0.00	1,019.86
19.	Nov. 2	3,186.13	8/10, 4/30, n/90	Dec. 28	0.00	3,186.13
20.	Dec. 16	5,190.60	4/10, 2/30, n/60	Jan. 10	103.81	5,086.79

Test 69

Name _____ Total Score _____

Date _____ Basic Score   100

Basic Time — 10 Minutes   Improvement Score _____

Solve these problems. Write the answers in the spaces on the right. (20 each)

1. An invoice for $896.49 is dated March 26 and has terms of 4/10, n/30. Find (a) the final date on which the cash discount may be taken and (b) the amount necessary to pay this invoice in full if the cash discount is earned. ....

   (a) _____
   (b) _____

2. An invoice totaling $475, terms 3/15, n/60, is dated March 30. Find (a) the final date on which the cash discount may be taken and (b) the amount that will pay the invoice in full if the cash discount is earned. ....

   (a) _____
   (b) _____

3. An invoice totaling $1,347.25 is dated May 22 and has terms of 3/10, 2/20, 1/40, n/70. How much would pay this invoice in full on June 11? ....

   _____

4. An invoice for $2,165 is dated December 15 and has terms of 4/30, 2/60, n/90. Find the amount necessary to pay this invoice in full on January 15. ....

   _____

5. On May 28 the R & B Company purchased raw materials invoiced at $3,558 with terms of 5/10, 2/30, n/60. The company paid the invoice in full, less the discount, on June 8. What was the amount of the payment? ....

   _____

6. The regular terms offered by the Cheviot Company are 3/10, 1/30, n/60. On June 17 Pamela Carr purchased merchandise worth $346.75 from the company. On June 27 she purchased merchandise worth $129.80. On July 7 she paid both invoices. What was the amount of the total payment? ....

   _____

7. On January 24 a merchant bought goods invoiced at $654.32, terms 2/10, n/30. The merchant returned part of the goods and received $65 credit for the return. On February 4 a check for the balance due was sent. What was the amount of the check? ....

   _____

8. An invoice for goods amounting to $1,441 was subject to discounts of 25%, 15%, and 10% with terms of 3/15, n/60. How much was the net cash price if paid within the discount period? ....

   _____

9. How much was paid for merchandise invoiced at $1,367 and subject to discounts of 25% and 10%, terms 2/10, n/30, if purchased on August 27 and paid for on September 6? ....

   _____

10. What is the least amount a merchant would have to pay for 25 lamps listed at $120 each if trade discounts of $33\frac{1}{3}$%, 10%, and 10% are allowed and if the terms are 4/10, 2/30, n/90? ....

    _____

Exercise 70

Discounts on Invoices

Invoices from wholesale houses often contain a variety of articles. Some of the articles are sold at certain rates of discount, while others are sold at different rates. Those articles having the same rates of trade discount are grouped together in order to save discount calculations. Total these net prices to obtain the net amount of the bill.

If a cash discount is allowed for payment within a certain time, figure the cash discount on the net amount of the bill and deduct it from the net amount. Determine due date by the exact-time method.

BASIC TIME — 12 Minutes *(Estimated time to obtain a basic score of 100)*

Figure the amount that will pay the following bill on January 31, 19--:

VIKING SUPPLIES, INC.
3460 Brady Street   Fort Worth, TX 76109-2525
Tel: (817) 379-0914

INVOICE No. 6406

SOLD TO Ms. Parma Samad
138 E. Berry Street
Fort Worth, TX 76110-4030

DATE January 5, 19--
TERMS 2/30, n/60

QUANTITY	DESCRIPTION	UNIT PRICE	AMOUNT	NET AMOUNT
3	Calculator (pocket)	$12.50		
4	Stapler	8.95	(8)	
	Less 10% and 5%		(30)	(4)
6 doz.	Writing pads	2.00		
10 doz.	Scratch pads	1.75		
5 doz.	Pencils (mechanical)	3.75		
3 doz.	Markers	4.65		
5 doz.	Pens (ballpoint)	5.10	(20)	(4)
	Less 20% and 10%		(20)	
325 sheets	Cardboard (per 100)	2.24		
275 sheets	Pressboard (per doz.)	1.80		
500 sheets	Paper (per 100)	4.75		
65 sheets	Cover (plastic)	0.19		
2	Binder	2.75		
25	Folder	0.50		
18	Lamp (desk)	19.50		
24	Tray (plastic)	1.75		
24	Labels	0.25	(72)	
	Less 25% and 20%		(16)	(4)
	Total of invoice		(10)	
	Less cash discount		(8)	
	Net amount paid		(4)	

Test 70

Name	Total Score	
Date	Basic Score	100
Basic Time — 12 Minutes	Improvement Score	

Figure the amount that will pay the following bill on December 28, 19--:

DATE December 18, 19--   INVOICE NO. 6613

TERMS 2/10, n/30

SOLD TO Mr. Arturo Herrera
1200 Madison Avenue
Syracuse, NY 13210-5325

PS PAPERWORKS SHOP
450 LAFAYETTE ROAD
SYRACUSE, NY 13205-6070
AREA CODE (315) 650-6000

QUANTITY	DESCRIPTION	UNIT PRICE	AMOUNT	AMOUNT
6 doz.	Markers	$ 6.50		
24	Pens (fine point)	4.00		
18 doz.	Pens (ballpoint)	5.25		
30 doz.	Pencils (lead)	1.35		
12	Pen & pencil sets	3.80	(16) _____	
	Less 20% and 5%		(22) _____	(4) _____
12	Ribbons (calculator)	1.45		
15	Ribbons (printer)	4.20	(8) _____	
	Less 15% and 10%		(26) _____	(4) _____
25	Pads (plastic)	0.50		
50	Pads (paper)	0.25	(8) _____	
	Less 10% and 10%		(18) _____	(4) _____
10	Notebook	2.75		
8	Binder (data)	2.50		
6	Binder (ring)	4.50		
12	Binder (pressboard)	3.40		
6	Binder (heavy duty)	5.25		
12	Labels	0.75		
36	Cover (report)	3.35	(30) _____	
	Less 20%, 10%, and 10%		(34) _____	(4) _____
	Total of invoice		(10)	_____
	Less cash discount		(8)	_____
	Net amount paid		(4)	_____

Exercise 71 — Simple Interest Formula

Interest is an amount paid for the use of money. A **bank discount** is interest collected in advance by a bank at the time money is borrowed from it.

In order to find the **ordinary simple interest** (or bank discount) on any sum of money for any length of time at any rate of interest, you may use the formula *Interest = Principal × Rate × Time in Years* or abbreviated as I = PRT. See Example A.

Example A   Find the interest on $900 at 6% for two years (I = PRT).

I = $900 × 0.06 × 2 = $108

Interest is charged on an annual basis. When the length of time of a loan is stated in months, the number of months is placed over 12. See Example B.

Example B   Find the interest on $900 at 6% for 3 months (I = PRT).

I = $900 × 0.06 × $\frac{3}{12}$ = $13.50

When time is expressed in days, the number of days is placed over 360, the *business-year basis* for computing ordinary interest. See Example C.

Example C   Find the interest on $900 at 6% for 90 days (I = PRT).

I = $900 × 0.06 × $\frac{90}{360}$ = $13.50

BASIC TIME — 18 Minutes *(Estimated time to obtain a basic score of 100)*

Find the ordinary simple interest for each of the following:

#	PRINCIPAL	RATE	YEARS	INTEREST	
1.	$725	6%	1	_____	(10)
2.		5%	2	_____	(10)
3.		8%	5	_____	(12)

#	PRINCIPAL	RATE	MONTHS	INTEREST	
4.	$3,500	8%	3	_____	(14)
5.		12%	5	_____	(12)
6.		10%	8	_____	(20)

#	PRINCIPAL	RATE	DAYS	INTEREST	
7.	$3,330	10%	60	_____	(10)
8.		9%	80	_____	(10)
9.		12%	36	_____	(10)

#	PRINCIPAL	RATE	DAYS	INTEREST	
10.	$925	8%	18	_____	(8)
11.		15%	53	_____	(16)
12.		9%	57	_____	(18)

13. What amount of interest would be earned on this note as of June 16, 1986? (Calculate the exact number of days through June 16; then use the 360-day business year for the interest calculation.)

_____ (30)

$1,250.00   Pittsburgh, Pa.   March 1, 1986
Six months AFTER DATE 1 PROMISE TO PAY TO
THE ORDER OF Charles M. Anderson
PAYABLE AT First National Bank
Twelve Hundred Fifty and 00/100 ---------- DOLLARS
VALUE RECEIVED WITH INTEREST AT 7%
No. 111   DUE _____
L. D. Frye

14. What amount of interest would be paid when this note is due? (Use the business-year basis for interest calculation.)

_____ (20)

$1,750.00   Chicago, Ill.   December 24, 1988
Sixty days AFTER DATE 1 PROMISE TO PAY TO
THE ORDER OF C. H. Kremer
PAYABLE AT First National Bank
One Thousand Seven Hundred Fifty and 00/100 -------- DOLLARS
VALUE RECEIVED WITH INTEREST AT 8%
No. 322   DUE _____
D. M. Ritter

144

Test 71

Name _____ Total Score _____
Date _____ Basic Score 100
Basic Time — 10 Minutes Improvement Score _____

1. Find the interest on the following note to maturity. (Use the business-year basis for the computation.) .... _____ (24)

$625.00   Atlanta, Georgia August 5, 19 88
Forty-five Days AFTER DATE I PROMISE TO PAY TO
THE ORDER OF _Friedman Tailors_
PAYABLE AT **Merchants Bank**
Six Hundred Twenty-five and 00/100 DOLLARS
VALUE RECEIVED WITH INTEREST AT _12%_
No. _222_ DUE _____
                    R. K. Ballister

On the above note, what would the interest have been:

2. At 7%? .... _____ (8) 3. At 8%? .... _____ (14)

4. At 10%? .... _____ (14) 5. At 14%? .... _____ (14)

6. Find the interest on the following note to maturity. (Calculate the exact number of days for maturity. Then use the business-year basis for the interest calculation.) .... _____ (50)

$1,760.00   Atlanta, Georgia February 15, 19 88
_____ AFTER DATE I PROMISE TO PAY TO
THE ORDER OF _The First National Bank_
PAYABLE AT **Merchants Bank**
One Thousand Seven Hundred Sixty and 00/100 DOLLARS
VALUE RECEIVED WITH INTEREST AT _9%_
No. _445_ DUE _June 30, 1988_
                    Mary Hart

On the above note, what would the interest have been:

7. At 10%? .... _____ (18) 8. At $14\frac{1}{2}$%? .... _____ (18)

9. At $7\frac{1}{2}$%? .... _____ (24) 10. At 18%? .... _____ (16)

Exercise 72 Compound Interest

Compound interest is computed on the sum of an original principal plus its accumulated interest. For example, money placed in a savings account at a bank will earn interest at a given rate. The bank adds the interest earned to the account periodically (monthly, or quarterly).

The added interest increases the balance in the account, which earns interest during the next period. Thus, interest added at the end of one period becomes principal in the next period. The sum of the original principal and its compound interest is the **compound amount**.

Example A Judy Kepler deposited $1,000 in a fund that pays 10% compounded annually. Find (a) the compound amount and (b) the compound interest at the end of two years.

Solution:
Original principal	$1,000
Interest for 1st period	100
Compound amount	$1,100
Interest for 2d period	110
(a) Compound amount	$1,210

(b) $1,210 − $1,000 = $210 compound interest

Example B Jack Pence deposited $1,000 in a fund that pays 10% compounded semiannually. Find the compound amount at the end of two years.

Solution:
Original principal	$1,000.00
Interest for 1st period	50.00
Compound amount	$1,050.00
Interest for 2d period	52.50
Compound amount	$1,102.50
Interest for 3d period	55.13
Compound amount	$1,157.63
Interest for 4th period	57.88
Compound amount	$1,215.51

BASIC TIME — 24 Minutes *(Estimated time to obtain a basic score of 100)*

For each problem, find (a) the compound amount and (b) the compound interest: (10 each answer)

	PRINCIPAL	RATE	TIME	COMPOUNDED	a COMPOUND AMOUNT	b COMPOUND INTEREST
1.	$ 800	15%	3 years	annually	_____	_____
2.	1,500	10%	4 years	annually	_____	_____
3.	7,000	14%	2 years	semiannually	_____	_____
4.	23,000	9%	2½ years	semiannually	_____	_____
5.	90,000	16%	1 year	quarterly	_____	_____
6.	64,000	12%	¼ year	monthly	_____	_____

Solve these problems. Place each answer in the appropriate space on the right. (10 each answer)

7. Leonard Drake deposited $30,000 in an account that pays 8% compounded quarterly. Find the compound amount at the end of one year................ _____

8. Matilda Johnson invested $25,000 in a certificate that paid 15% compounded monthly. How much interest did this certificate earn in four months?.......... _____

9. Four years ago a trust fund of $50,000 was invested at 12.5% compounded annually. Find the amount in the fund now............ _____

10. Jesse Williams inherited $75,000 on the day he became twenty-one years old. The money was placed in a trust fund that earned interest at 15% compounded semiannually. What amount was in the fund on his twenty-third birthday?............. _____

11. Fifteen months ago the original amount in a fund was $15,000. The interest rate is 12%. Find (a) the simple interest and (b) the interest compounded quarterly. ...
(a) _____
(b) _____

12. The sum of $46,000 was invested at 18% compounded monthly. (a) How much was in the fund at the end of three months? (b) How much more was earned with compound interest than would have been earned with simple interest?................
(a) _____
(b) _____

Test 72

Name _____ **Total Score** _____

Date _____ **Basic Score** __100__

Basic Time — 21 Minutes **Improvement Score** _____

For each problem, find (a) the compound amount and (b) the compound interest: (10 each answer)

	PRINCIPAL	RATE	TIME	COMPOUNDED	a COMPOUND AMOUNT	b COMPOUND INTEREST
1.	$ 700	9%	3 years	annually	_____	_____
2.	2,400	8%	1 year	quarterly	_____	_____
3.	9,000	14%	1½ years	semiannually	_____	_____
4.	25,000	15%	¼ year	monthly	_____	_____
5.	80,000	11%	2 years	semiannually	_____	_____
6.	36,000	18%	⅓ year	monthly	_____	_____

Solve these problems. Write each answer in the appropriate space on the right. (10 each answer)

7. Wilma Conci deposited $40,000 in an account that pays 9% compounded monthly. How much compound interest did this account earn in three months?.... _____

8. Charles Struble invested $32,000 in a certificate that paid 14% compounded quarterly. Find the compound amount at the end of nine months............................ _____

9. Two years ago a trust fund of $60,000 was invested at 13% compounded semi-annually. Find the amount in the fund now. .... _____

10. Lucille Odum inherited $85,000 on the day she became eighteen years old. The money was placed in a trust fund that earned interest at 14% compounded annually. What amount was in the fund on her twenty-first birthday?........................ _____

11. Five months ago the amount in a fund was $43,000. The interest rate is 12%. Find (a) the simple interest and (b) the interest compounded monthly...................
   (a) _____
   (b) _____

12. The sum of $27,000 was invested at 16% compounded quarterly. (a) How much was in the fund at the end of one year? (b) How much more was earned with compound interest than would have been earned with simple interest?.................
   (a) _____
   (b) _____

Exercise 73 Application Problems

BASIC TIME — 16 Minutes *(Estimated time to obtain a basic score of 100)*

Solve these problems. Write the answers in the spaces on the right. (10 each, Nos. 1–16)

1. How much is 32% of $92.10? .... _____

2. What is 18% of 41? .... _____

3. What percent of 132 is 231? .... _____

4. 125 is 25% of what number? .... _____

5. Find the interest on $8,525 at 6% for 6 months. .... _____

6. Find the interest on $1,215 at $10\frac{1}{2}$% for 1 year. .... _____

7. Find the interest on $675 at 8% for 180 days. .... _____

8. Find the interest on $540 at 12% for 90 days. .... _____

9. Find the compound interest on $4,000 at 14% compounded quarterly for 1 year. . _____

10. Find the compound amount on $7,500 at $8\frac{1}{2}$% compounded annually for 3 years. _____

11. Find the interest at $14\frac{1}{2}$% on $8,450 for 45 days. .... _____

12. Find the interest on $896.50 at 15% for 60 days. .... _____

13. Find the amount to be paid on an invoice for $340.78, terms 6/10, 3/30, n/60, which was dated September 26 and paid on October 26. .... _____

14. Lew was born on April 18, 1970. His brother David was born on June 4, 1973. How much older is Lew than David? (*Use the compound method.*) .... _____

15. Amelia Lugo wishes to save $7,500 in one year for her vacation. If her annual salary is $30,000, what percent of it should she save for the vacation? .... _____

16. An agent sells merchandise on 15% commission. What is the total sales value of the merchandise that must be sold in order to earn $600 in commission? .... _____

17. An agent sold 750 crates of produce for a grower at $7.65 each and 157 crates at $7.50 each. The agent paid storage charges of $37.49 and freight charges of $72.89. How much net proceeds were due the grower if the agent's commission rate was $4\frac{1}{2}$%? .... _____(25)

18. How much was paid for merchandise purchased on September 23, invoiced at $1,385, subject to trade discounts of 30% and 20%, terms 2/10, n/30, and paid for on October 3? .... _____(15)

148

Test 73

Name _____ Total Score _____

Date _____ Basic Score   100

Basic Time — 16 Minutes Improvement Score _____

Solve these problems. Write the answers in the spaces on the right. (10 each, Nos. 1–14)

1. What is 2.3% of 89? .... _____

2. 85 is 20% of what amount? .... _____

3. What percent of $947 is $217.81? .... _____

4. What number is 23% of $875? .... _____

5. Find the interest on $9,767.75 at $10\frac{1}{2}$% for 240 days. .... _____

6. Find the interest at $12\frac{1}{4}$% on $750 for 1 year. .... _____

7. Find the interest at $9\frac{1}{4}$% on $1,750 for 30 days. .... _____

8. Find the interest on $1,250 at 15% for 4 months. .... _____

9. Find the compound amount on $9,000 at 12% compounded semiannually for 2 years. .... _____

10. How much is the compound interest on $6,000 for 3 months at 18% compounded monthly? .... _____

11. Find the amount to be paid on an invoice for $917.23, terms 4/10, 2/30, n/60, dated on July 16, and paid on August 16. .... _____

12. A student traveled in Europe from June 16 to October 8. The student was in Europe for exactly how many days? .... _____

13. An automobile traveling at 60 miles per hour moves at a speed of 5,280 feet a minute. How far will it move in 35 seconds? .... _____

14. Jana Koshinski received a salary of $295 a week plus a commission of 5% on all goods sold over $1,500 in a week. If $3,343.58 worth of goods were sold during one week, what was Jana's total salary that week? .... _____

15. A commission merchant bought and shipped to a Denver company 375 boxes of a product at $6.95 a box and 250 boxes at $5.80 a box. Charges were $47.25 for storage and $108.59 for freight. If the rate of commission was $6\frac{1}{2}$%, how much gross cost was paid by the Denver company? .... _____(40)

16. A merchant purchased 75 radios listed at $48 each. Special trade discounts were as follows: $16\frac{2}{3}$%, $12\frac{1}{2}$%, and 20%; terms 5/10, 2/20, n/60. What is the least that must be paid? .... _____(20)

Exercise 74 — U. S. Measurements

In this exercise, common measurements are given. Review thoroughly the list of equivalent values presented in the right-hand column below.

The problems to be solved require that measurements in one denomination be changed to equivalent higher or lower denominations.

You may need scratch paper for figuring. Write each answer in the space allotted, and show any remainder as a fractional part in lowest terms.

Example
How many minutes are there in 260 seconds?
Solution: 60 seconds = 1 minute
Therefore: 260 seconds ÷ 60 seconds = $4\frac{20}{60}$ minutes = $4\frac{1}{3}$ minutes

---

BASIC TIME — 7 Minutes *(Estimated time to obtain a basic score of 100)*

Supply the required answers as indicated: (8 each)

1. 768 inches = _____ feet
2. 102 feet = _____ yards
3. 7,920 feet = _____ miles
4. 340 seconds = _____ minutes
5. 843 minutes = _____ hours
6. 1,020 hours = _____ days
7. 4,160 days = _____ weeks
8. 1,095 days = _____ years
9. 792 months = _____ years
10. 728 weeks = _____ years
11. 864 sq. inches = _____ square feet
12. 801 sq. feet = _____ square yards
13. 5,760 acres = _____ square miles
14. 15,552 cu. inches = _____ cubic feet
15. 351 cu. feet = _____ cubic yards
16. 1,060 fl. ounces = _____ quarts
17. 483 pints = _____ quarts
18. 528 quarts = _____ gallons
19. 2,079 cu. inches = _____ gallons
20. 216 articles = _____ dozen
21. 468 dozen = _____ gross
22. 1,152 articles = _____ gross
23. 1,248 ounces = _____ pounds
24. 9,000 pounds = _____ tons
25. 60 mills = _____ cents

```
12 in. = 1 ft.
3 ft. = 1 yd.
5,280 ft. = 1 mi.
60 sec. = 1 min.
60 min. = 1 hr.
24 hours = 1 day
7 days = 1 wk.
365 days = 1 yr.
12 mo. = 1 yr.
52 wk. = 1 yr.
144 sq. in. = 1 sq. ft.
9 sq. ft. = 1 sq. yd.
640 acres = 1 sq. mi.
1,728 cu. in. = 1 cu. ft.
27 cu. ft. = 1 cu. yd.
32 fl. oz. = 1 qt.
2 pt. = 1 qt.
4 qt. = 1 gal.
231 cu. in. = 1 gal.
12 articles = 1 doz.
12 doz. = 1 gr.
144 articles = 1 gr.
16 oz. = 1 lb.
2,000 lb. = 1 T.
10 mills = 1 cent
```

150

Test 74

Name _____ Total Score _____
Date _____ Basic Score __100__
Basic Time — 9 Minutes Improvement Score _____

Solve these problems. Write the answers in the spaces on the right. (20 each)

1. A stationer sold 7 gross of pencils at 2 pencils for 5 cents. What was the total amount received for the pencils? .... _____

2. A wheel, 15 feet in circumference, makes how many revolutions in going one mile? .... _____

3. How many days are there in 80 hours? .... _____

4. How many square yards of carpet will cover a floor containing 117 square feet? .... _____

5. A bridge abutment contains 3,888 cubic feet. How many cubic yards are there in it? .... _____

6. How many pieces of tile of 24 square inches each will cover 336 square feet of floor? .... _____

7. How many yards of tape are required for 28 pieces of 27 inches each? .... _____

8. How many posts, 3 yards apart, will be needed for a fence around an estate 3 miles around? .... _____

9. How many hours are there in 230,400 seconds? .... _____

10. How many weeks are there in 525 days? .... _____

Exercise 75 — Denominate Numbers

Numbers such as 6, $3\frac{1}{2}$, and 7.5 that do not refer to objects are **abstract numbers**. Numbers that do refer to objects, such as 6 pencils, $3\frac{1}{2}$ pies, and 8.5 gallons, are **concrete numbers**. Concrete numbers that are expressed in terms of standard units of measure are **denominate numbers**. For example, 5 dollars, 6 weeks, $7\frac{1}{4}$ pounds, and 8.5 gallons are denominate numbers; they identify the measures of quantity.

To add or subtract denominate numbers, arrange the numbers in columns with the lowest denomination on the right so that like denominations will be added or subtracted.

Example A Add: 6 yd. 1 ft. 8 in.
                    3 yd. 2 ft. 7 in.
                   10 yd. 1 ft. 3 in.

Solution A. Add 8 in. and 7 in. obtaining 15 in., or 1 ft. and 3 in. Write 3 under the inches column and carry 1 to the next column to the left, the total of which becomes 4 ft. As 4 ft. make 1 yd. and 1 ft., write 1 under the feet column and carry 1 to the next column, the total of which becomes 10 yd.

Example B Subtract:
              4   89
              5̸ hr. 3̸0 min. 2̸0 80 sec.
              3 hr. 45 min. 30 sec.
              1 hr. 44 min. 50 sec.

Solution B. Borrow 1 min. from the 30 min. to make 29 min. and 80 sec. Subtract 30 sec. from 80 sec. and write the difference, 50 sec., in the "seconds" column. Borrow 1 hr. from the 5 hr. to give 4 hr. 89 min. Subtract 45 min. from 89 min. and 3 hr. from 4 hr. Write the answers in the appropriate columns.

BASIC TIME — 7 Minutes *(Estimated time to obtain a basic score of 100)*

Add: (20 each)

1. 6 days   4 hr.   15 min.
    5 "   3 "   24 "
    7 "   11 "   17 "
    2 "   10 "   5 "

2. $7   8 ct.   4 mills
    4   37 "   9 "
   12   84 "   6 "
    3   26 "   8 "

3. 16 hr. 11 min. 20 sec.
   12 "   29 "   16 "
    3 "   15 "   25 "
    6 "   18 "   18 "

4. 25 gr. 10 doz. 4 art.
    2 "   11 "   8 "
    3 "   9 "   6 "
   12 "   8 "   7 "

Subtract: (20 each)

5. 6 gal. 1 qt. 0 pt.
   3 "   3 "   1 "

6. 76 cu. yd. 8 cu. ft. 100 cu. in.
   75 " "   8 " "   121 " "

7. 7 yr.   9 wk.   6 da.
   3 "   12 "   9 "

8. 16 sq. yd. 2 sq. ft. 12 sq. in.
   15 " "   8 " "   27 " "

9. 10 yd. 1 ft. 10 in.
    4 "   2 "   11 "

10. 24 hr. 1 min. 5 sec.
    17 "   5 "   7 "

Test 75

Name ___
Date ___
Basic Time — 5 Minutes

Total Score ___
Basic Score 100
Improvement Score ___

Add: (20 each)

1. 25 gr.   10 doz.   9 art
    12 "   11 "   10 "
    11 "   5 "   9 "
     5 "   9 "   11 "
    ———————————————————

4. 1 yd.   2 ft.   11 in.
    2 "   1 "   8 "
                     2 "   7 "
    6 "   10 "
    ———————————————————

2. 12 hr.   14 min.   14 sec.
     7 "   10 "   38 "
     3 "   18 "   20 "
     1 "   19 "   23 "
    ———————————————————

5. 2 sq. yd.   8 sq. ft.   120 sq. in.
    3 " "   5 " "   82 " "
    6 " "   7 " "   57 " "
    1 " "   2 " "   13 " "
    ———————————————————

3. 11 yr.   10 mo.
    10 "   8 "
     9 "   8 "
     7 "   4 "
    ———————————————————

6. 9 gal.   3 qt.   1 pt.
    15 "   2 "
    17 "   1 "   1 "
     7 "   1 "
    ———————————————————

Subtract: (20 each)

7. 20 lb.   14 oz.
    12 "   15 "
    ———————————————————

9. 1,927 days   4 hr.   16 min.
    1,921 "   5 "   24 "
    ———————————————————

8. 7 yr.   10 wk.   14 da.
    2 "   15 "   18 "
    ———————————————————

10. 17 gr.   4 doz.   6 art.
    11 "   9 "   11 "
    ———————————————————

Exercise 76: Vocabulary of Metric System of Measurement

The metric system of measuring length, capacity, weight, and area is used in science and industry in the United States and is the official system that is used in most countries of the world. The names of the units of measure commonly used in the metric system are as follows:

Name	Pronunciation	Meaning
meter (m)	*meeter*	unit of length
liter (L)	*leeter*	unit of capacity
gram (g)	*gram*	unit of weight

Prefixes are added to the foregoing names to indicate 10, 100, or 1,000 (and other powers of 10) times the unit of measure being used. For example, **deka**liter means 10 liters, **hecto**gram means 100 grams, and **kilo**meter means 1,000 meters. Likewise, other prefixes may be appended to each name of a unit of measure to show 0.1, 0.01, or 0.001 part of. Notice that **deci**gram means 0.1 gram; **centi**meter, 0.01 meter; and **milli**liter, 0.001 liter. A space, rather than a comma is used to separate large numbers into groups of three. A zero is always used before a decimal point.

Prefix	Meaning	Numerical Value
kilo (k)	one thousand times	1 000
hecto (h)	one hundred times	100
deka (da)	ten times	10
	base unit (meter, liter, gram)	1
deci (d)	one tenth part of	0.1
centi (c)	one hundredth part of	0.01
milli (m)	one thousandth part of	0.001

BASIC TIME — 2 Minutes (*Estimated time to obtain a basic score of 100*)

In the appropriate space on the right, place the name or prefix that is asked for in each question. Do not abbreviate. (20 each)

1. What name is applied to the standard unit of measure for length in the metric system? .... _____

2. In the metric system of measurement, what is the name of the standard unit of measure for weight? .... _____

3. In the metric system, what is the name of the standard unit of measure for capacity? .... _____

4. What is used instead of the comma to separate large numbers into groups of three in the metric system? .... _____

5. What prefix is used in the metric system to mean one thousandth part of? .... _____

6. In the metric system, what is the prefix that is used to mean ten times? .... _____

7. What prefix is used in the metric system to mean one tenth part of? .... _____

8. In the metric system, what prefix is used to mean one thousand times? .... _____

9. In the metric system, what prefix is used to mean one hundredth part of? .... _____

10. What is the prefix that is used in the metric system to mean one hundred times? .... _____

Test 76

Name _____ Total Score _____

Date _____ Basic Score ___100___

Basic Time — 2 Minutes Improvement Score _____

Place each answer in the appropriate space on the right. Do not abbreviate. (20 each)

1. In the metric system of measurement, what is the name of the standard unit of measure for weight?.. _____

2. What name is applied to the standard unit of measure for capacity in the metric system?.. _____

3. In the metric system, what is the name of the standard unit of measure for length?. _____

4. What prefix is used in the metric system to mean one hundredth part of?............... _____

5. What prefix is used in the metric system to mean one thousandth part of?............. _____

6. In the metric system, what prefix is used to mean one thousand times?................. _____

7. What prefix is used in the metric system to mean one tenth part of? .... _____

8. What is the prefix that is used in the metric system of measurement to mean one hundred times?.. _____

9. In the metric system, what prefix is used to mean 10 times?................................... _____

10. Write the number ten thousand as it appears in the metric system. .... _____

Exercise 77 Metric Measurements

Changing from a metric unit of measurement to a larger or smaller metric unit may be done by moving the decimal point to the left or right. Using a chart like the one shown in the examples simplifies the procedure. The prefixes in the chart are arranged in order of size.

To change a metric unit to a larger metric unit, move the decimal point one place to the left for each higher unit.

Example A shows that deka is *four* places to the left of milli. To change the milli units to deka units, the point is moved four places to the left.

To change a metric unit to a smaller metric unit, move the decimal point one place to the right for each lower unit.

Example B shows that deci is *two* places to the *right* of grams. Therefore, the decimal point is moved two places to the right.

Example A Change 8 000 millimeters to dekameters.

Base

kilo hecto deka Unit deci centi milli

Solution: 8 000 mm = 8 000 dam = 0.8 dam

Example B Change 700 grams to centigrams.

Base

kilo hecto deka Unit deci centi milli

Solution: 700 g = 700.00 cg = 70 000 cg

meters (m)		liters (L)		grams (g)	
kilometer (km) =	1 000 m	kiloliter (kL) =	1 000 L	kilogram (kg) =	1 000 g
hectometer (hm) =	100 m	hectoliter (hL) =	100 L	hectogram (hg) =	100 g
dekameter (dam) =	10 m	dekaliter (daL) =	10 L	dekagram (dag) =	10 g
meter (m) =	1 m	liter (L) =	1 L	gram (g) =	1 g
decimeter (dm) =	0.1 m	deciliter (dL) =	0.1 L	decigram (dg) =	0.1 g
centimeter (cm) =	0.01 m	centiliter (cL) =	0.01 L	centigram (cg) =	0.01 g
millimeter (mm) =	0.001 m	milliliter (mL) =	0.001 L	milligram (mg) =	0.001 g

BASIC TIME — 12 Minutes *(Estimated time to obtain a basic score of 100)*

Write the full name for each of the following symbols: (10 each)

1. 3 kg _____
2. 2 mL _____
3. 1 cm _____
4. 3 dm _____
5. 1 g _____
6. 6 L _____

Change the metric values below as indicated: (10 each)

SMALLER TO LARGER

7. 40 mm = _____ cm
8. 69 g = _____ dag
9. 400 cg = _____ dg
10. 20 dm = _____ m
11. 30 mm = _____ dm
12. 300 L = _____ kL
13. 20 g = _____ kg

LARGER TO SMALLER

14. 2 cL = _____ mL
15. 15 kg = _____ hg
16. 5 L = _____ dL
17. 6 dm = _____ cm
18. 4 g = _____ cg
19. 2 km = _____ dam
20. 4 kg = _____ g

Test 77

Name _____ Total Score _____

Date _____ Basic Score   100

Basic Time — 12 Minutes Improvement Score _____

Write the full name for each of the following symbols: (10 each)

1. 1 mm _____ 4. 3 hg _____

2. 1 dag _____ 5. 1 km _____

3. 3 cL _____ 6. 1 dL _____

Change the metric values below as indicated: (10 each)

7. 4 mm = _____ cm 14. 0.001 m = _____ dm

8. 300 g = _____ kg 15. 0.1 g = _____ dg

9. 4 L = _____ cL 16. 90 L = _____ hL

10. 20 km = _____ dam 17. 7 daL = _____ hL

11. 8 dL = _____ mL 18. 600 m = _____ km

12. 60 g = _____ dag 19. 3 dg = _____ cg

13. 4 kL = _____ L 20. 80 hL = _____ kL

Exercise 78 — Metric Denominates

Metric denominates are added, subtracted, multiplied, and divided just like any other values, but they must always be expressed in equivalent units before any calculations are made.

In Examples A and B the metric denominates are changed to equivalent units before the addition or subtraction. If decimals are involved, the values must be aligned on the decimal points.

In Examples C and D the multiplication and division of the metric denominates proceed in the usual way. The answers are expressed in the metric unit of measure that is used.

Example A   Add 6.5 meters and 35 centimeters.

Solution: Change the 35 centimeters to 0.35 meter. Then add the meters:

$$\begin{array}{r} 6.5 \text{ m} \\ +0.35 \text{ m} \\ \hline 6.85 \text{ m} \end{array}$$

Example B   Subtract 125 millimeters from 75 centimeters.

Solution: Change 125 millimeters to 12.5 centimeters. Then subtract:

$$\begin{array}{r} 75.0 \text{ cm} \\ -12.5 \text{ cm} \\ \hline 62.5 \text{ cm} \end{array}$$

Example C   Multiply 12.3 meters by 5.

Solution:

$$\begin{array}{r} 12.3 \text{ m} \\ \times \quad 5 \\ \hline 61.5 \text{ m} \end{array}$$

Example D   Divide 620 millimeters by 4.

Solution: $4\overline{)620}$ mm $= 155$ mm

BASIC TIME — 6 Minutes *(Estimated time to obtain a basic score of 100)*

Add: (12 each)

1. 50 mL + 625 mL + 325 mL = _____ mL
2. 40 g + 0.9 kg = _____ g
3. 30 km + 5 m = _____ km
4. 35.2 L + 3.75 L + 7.945 L = _____ L
5. 6 g + 20 dg = _____ g

Subtract: (12 each)

6. 5 g − 1 mg = _____ g
7. 5 m − 15 mm = _____ m
8. 85 cm − 150 mm = _____ cm
9. 7 dL − 60 mL = _____ dL
10. 6 g − 600 mg = _____ g

Multiply: (8 each)

11. 345 L × 20 = _____ L
12. 0.36 kL × 8 = _____ kL
13. 0.75 g × 1.5 = _____ g
14. 0.6 mm × 268 = _____ mm
15. 55 kg × 1.5 = _____ kg

Divide: (8 each)

16. 39 L ÷ 3 = _____ L
17. 625.5 kg ÷ 5 = _____ kg
18. 1 004 m ÷ 8 = _____ m
19. 876 mg ÷ 24 = _____ mg
20. 333.2 mL ÷ 14 = _____ mL

Test 78

Name _____ Total Score _____
Date _____ Basic Score   100
Basic Time — 12 Minutes Improvement Score _____

Add: (6 each)

1. 6 dg + 15 dg + 253 dg = _____ dg
2. 82.25 g + 46.037 g = _____ g
3. 75 cL + 4.5 L = _____ cL
4. 350 cm + 8.75 m = _____ m
5. 18 daL + 30 L = _____ daL
6. 6 m + 48 mm = _____ mm
7. 54 g + 1.2 hg = _____ hg
8. 2.4 L + 10.8 dL = _____ L
9. 38 dag + 648 g = _____ dag
10. 2.3 km + 728 m = _____ km

Multiply: (4 each)

21. 150 g × 6 = _____ g
22. 43 m × 18 = _____ m
23. 48.6 L × 9 = _____ L
24. 74 hL × 16 = _____ hL
25. 13 cm × 25 = _____ cm
26. 15.3 × 31 mg = _____ mg
27. 9.4 × 4.86 dL = _____ dL
28. 2.5 × 36 km = _____ km
29. 64 × 6.25 dag = _____ dag
30. 24 × 12.5 cL = _____ cL

Subtract: (6 each)

11. 34 m − 47 dm = _____ m
12. 125 g − 8 dag = _____ g
13. 768 L − 6 hL = _____ L
14. 27 dL − 8.1 mL = _____ dL
15. 4.3 g − 9.7 mg = _____ mg
16. 218.7 m − 1 hm = _____ hm
17. 65.6 m − 165 cm = _____ cm
18. 19.6 hg − 683 g = _____ g
19. 59.04 kL − 54.9 hL = _____ kL
20. 1 771 cm − 1.25 m = _____ m

Divide: (4 each)

31. 318 L ÷ 4 = _____ L
32. 864 m ÷ 8 = _____ m
33. 6 459.6 g ÷ 12 = _____ g
34. 956 dg ÷ 5 = _____ dg
35. 6 598.9 mm ÷ 11 = _____ mm
36. 39 L ÷ 6 = _____ L
37. 91.492 dam ÷ 8.9 = _____ dam
38. 7.14 kg ÷ 3.5 = _____ kg
39. 93.6 dL ÷ 7.8 = _____ dL
40. 520.56 hg ÷ 9.64 = _____ hg

Exercise 79

Converting from U. S. Measurements to Metric Measurements

United States units of measure may be changed to metric units of measure by multiplying the number of U. S. units by the equivalent of 1 metric unit in the measurement desired. The procedure may be accomplished in two steps:

1. Determine the metric equivalent of 1 unit of the U. S. measurement that is to be changed. (The equivalent metric unit is called the **conversion factor**.)
2. Multiply the conversion factor by the quantity to be changed.

Sometimes the decimal point in the conversion factor that is found in the table must be moved to the right or to the left. Notice in Example B that 1 inch equals 2.540 centimeters. As a centimeter is 0.01 meter, 2.540 centimeters equal 0.0254 meter (the conversion factor).

Example A	3 quarts =	? liters
Solution:	1 quart = 0.9463 liter (Table I)	
Therefore:	3 qt. = 3 × 0.9463 L = 2.8389 L	
Example B	50 inches =	? meters
Solution:	1 inch = 2.540 cm = 0.0254 meter	
Therefore:	50 in. = 50 × 0.0254 = 1.27 m	

BASIC TIME — 20 Minutes *(Estimated time to obtain a basic score of 100)*

Use Table I on page 165 to solve these problems. Where applicable, round the answer to the nearest ten-thousandth. Place each answer in the appropriate space on the right. (10 each)

1. 5 feet = _____ meters
2. 20 ounces = _____ grams
3. 12 liquid quarts = _____ liters
4. 23 acres = _____ hectares
5. 75 inches = _____ centimeters
6. 3 pounds = _____ grams
7. 56 fluidounces = _____ milliliters
8. 6 cubic feet = _____ cubic meters
9. 30 miles = _____ kilometers
10. 9 liquid pints = _____ liters
11. 7 short tons = _____ metric tons
12. 60 fluidounces = _____ liters
13. 25 gallons = _____ dekaliters
14. 15 inches = _____ meters
15. 40 pounds = _____ kilograms
16. 45 long tons = _____ metric tons
17. 35 inches = _____ decimeters
18. 9 ounces = _____ centigrams
19. 27 cubic inches = _____ cubic centimeters
20. 50 square feet = _____ square meters

Test 79

160

Name _____ Total Score _____
Date _____ Basic Score __100__
Basic Time — 18 Minutes   Improvement Score _____

Use Table I on page 165 to solve these problems. Where applicable, round the answer to the nearest ten-thousandth. Place each answer in the appropriate space on the right. (10 each)

1. 50 fluidounces = _____ milliliters
2. 12 pounds = _____ grams
3. 60 inches = _____ centimeters
4. 5 acres = _____ hectares
5. 15 liquid quarts = _____ liters
6. 18 ounces = _____ grams
7. 27 feet = _____ meters
8. 30 acres = _____ hectares
9. 17 liquid pints = _____ liters
10. 56 miles = _____ kilometers
11. 40 fluidounces = _____ liters
12. 6 short tons = _____ metric tons
13. 4 ounces = _____ centigrams
14. 70 inches = _____ decimeters
15. 37 long tons = _____ metric tons
16. 48 pounds = _____ kilograms
17. 26 inches = _____ meters
18. 45 pounds = _____ dekagrams
19. 32 square feet = _____ square meters
20. 28 cubic inches = _____ cubic centimeters

Exercise 80: Converting from Metric Measurements to U. S. Measurements

Metric units of measurement may be changed to U. S. measurements by multiplying the given number of metric units by the equivalent of 1 U. S. unit in the measurement desired. Follow these two steps:

1. Find the U. S. equivalent of 1 unit of the metric measurement that is to be changed. (The U. S. equivalent unit is the **conversion factor**.)
2. Multiply the quantity to be changed by the conversion factor.

On occasion, the desired conversion factor may be obtained by moving the decimal point in some other factor found in the table. Observe that in Example B, the conversion factor (3.28084 ft.) for one meter is obtained by moving the decimal point in the equivalent in feet of one dekameter (32.8084 ft.).

Example A Five liters equal how many liquid quarts?
Solution: 1 liter = 1.0567 quarts (Table II)
Therefore: 5 L = 5 × 1.0567 qt.
= 5.2835 qt.

Example B How many feet are there in 6 meters?
Solution: 1 dekameter = 32.8084 ft. (Table II)
1 meter = 3.28084 ft.
Therefore: 6 m = 6 × 3.28084 ft.
= 19.6850 ft.

BASIC TIME — 20 Minutes *(Estimated time to obtain a basic score of 100)*

Use Table II on page 167 to solve these problems. Where applicable, round the answer to the nearest ten-thousandth. Place each answer in the appropriate space on the right. (10 each)

1. Seven liters equal how many liquid quarts? _____
2. Five grams equal how many ounces? _____
3. Twelve square meters equal how many square yards? _____
4. How many inches are there in 4 meters? _____
5. How many pounds are there in 65 grams? _____
6. How many liquid pints are there in 9 liters? _____
7. There are how many acres in 3 hectares? _____
8. There are how many miles in 25 kilometers? _____
9. There are how many feet in 40 meters? _____
10. Twenty hectares equal how many acres? _____
11. Thirty square centimeters equal how many square inches? _____
12. Fourteen square meters equal how many square feet? _____
13. How many short tons are there in 17 metric tons? _____
14. How many fluidounces are there in 44 milliliters? _____
15. There are how many fluidrams in 75 centiliters? _____
16. There are how many yards in 130 meters? _____
17. Nineteen kilograms equal how many pounds? _____
18. Sixty dekameters equal how many feet? _____
19. How many square miles are there in 18 square kilometers? _____
20. How many ounces are there in 3 decigrams? _____

Test 80

Name _____ **Total Score** _____

Date _____ **Basic Score** ___100___

Basic Time — 8 Minutes **Improvement Score** _____

Use Table II on page 167 to solve these problems. Where applicable, round the answer to the nearest ten-thousandth. Place each answer in the appropriate space on the right. (10 each)

1. There are how many ounces in 9 grams? .... _____

2. There are how many acres in 15 hectares? .... _____

3. Eleven meters equal how many inches? .... _____

4. Seventy-one grams equal how many pounds? .... _____

5. Fifteen liters equal how many gallons? .... _____

6. How many square inches are there in 36 square centimeters? ..... _____

7. How many square yards are there in 5 square meters? .... _____

8. How many liquid pints are there in 3 liters? .... _____

9. How many acres are there in 12 hectares? .... _____

10. How many feet are there in 25 meters? .... _____

11. Forty kilometers equal how many miles? .... _____

12. Twenty liters equal how many liquid quarts? .... _____

13. How many fluidrams are there in 45 centiliters? .... _____

14. How many square feet are there in 24 square meters? .... _____

15. There are how many U. S. tons in 19 metric tons? .... _____

16. There are how many fluidounces in 37 milliliters? .... _____

17. How many inches are there in 625 centimeters? .... _____

18. How many pounds are there in 32 dekagrams? .... _____

19. Thirty-five decimeters equal how many inches? .... _____

20. Fifty square kilometers equal how many square miles? .... _____

POSTTEST   Name _____   Total Score _____
Date _____   Hour _____

These problems are very similar to those on the Pretest. In most cases, only the numbers have been changed. Place each answer in the appropriate space on the right. Show common fractions in lowest terms. (Score 2 points for each correct answer to Problems 1 through 20 and 3 points for each correct answer to Problems 21 through 40.)

Add:

1. 564
   320
   179
   428
   735

2. $2.70 + 4.35 + 0.09 + 7.98 =$

3. $\dfrac{5}{14}$
   $\dfrac{4}{7}$

4. $23\dfrac{7}{8}$
   $6\dfrac{11}{24}$

Subtract:

5. 6,700
   3,568

6. $8.34 - 5.792 =$

7. $\dfrac{11}{12} - \dfrac{2}{3} =$

8. $9\dfrac{7}{16}$
   $4\dfrac{5}{8}$

Multiply:

9. 685
   308

10. $\dfrac{5}{6} \times 45 =$

11. $\dfrac{8}{15} \times \dfrac{4}{9} =$

12. $16\dfrac{3}{4}$
    $4\dfrac{2}{5}$

13. $80 \times 0.80 =$

14. $3.6 \times 0.7 =$

Divide:

15. $648 \div 6 =$

16. $0.502 \div 0.004 =$

17. $24 \div \dfrac{5}{8} =$

18. $\dfrac{7}{8} \div \dfrac{3}{4} =$

19. $12\dfrac{1}{7} \div 17 =$

20. $3\dfrac{7}{12} \div 5\dfrac{3}{8} =$

(continued)

1. _____
2. _____
3. _____
4. _____
5. _____
6. _____
7. _____
8. _____
9. _____
10. _____
11. _____
12. _____
13. _____
14. _____
15. _____
16. _____
17. _____
18. _____
19. _____
20. _____

POSTTEST (concluded)

Write each of the following as a percent:

21. 0.0875
22. $\frac{3}{4}$
23. 6

Write each of the following as a common fraction:

24. 40%
25. $16\frac{2}{3}$%
26. $\frac{1}{4}$%

Write each of the following as a decimal fraction:

27. $1\frac{5}{8}$
28. $37\frac{1}{2}$%

29. Find the average of these daily attendance numbers:

   1,879   1,785   1,862   1,906   1,873   1,891

30. Solve this equation: $4(n + 3) - 2(n - 5) = 140$

Solve each of the following:

31. $12\frac{1}{2}$% of 320 = ___?___
32. 20 = 4% of ___?___
33. 12 = ___?___ % of 36

34. Subtract: 8 hr. 35 min.
             3 hr. 48 min.
35. 4,586 mm = ___?___ m

36. An agent sold a client's shipment of fruit and collected $2,486. The charges were $98.75 for freight and 7% commission for selling. How much should the agent send to the client?

37. A dealer listed terms of 3/10, n/30 on an invoice for $1,200 worth of goods. How much should the customer pay on June 13 for goods purchased on June 4?

38. Find the net price for merchandise listed on an invoice at $600 less trade discounts of 25% and 10%.

39. How much is the simple interest on $900 at 15% for ten months?

40. A student deposited $800 in an account that pays 10% interest compounded semiannually. Find the compound amount at the end of two years.

21. _____
22. _____
23. _____
24. _____
25. _____
26. _____
27. _____
28. _____
29. _____
30. _____
31. _____
32. _____
33. _____
34. _____
35. _____
36. _____
37. _____
38. _____
39. _____
40. _____

Table I

U. S. Units of Measure and Their Approximate Metric Equivalents

Cubic

1 cubic inch (cu. in. or in³) = 16.3871 cubic centimeters (cm³)
1 cubic foot (cu. ft. or ft³) = 0.0283 cubic meter (m³) = 28.316 liters (L)
1 cubic yard (cu. yd. or yd³) = 0.7646 cubic meter

Dry

1 pint (pt.)   = 33.6003 cubic inches (cu. in.) = 0.5506 liter (L)
1 quart (qt.) = 67.2006 cubic inches   = 1.1012 liters
1 peck (pk.)   = 537.605 cubic inches   = 8.8095 liters
1 bushel (bu.) = 2,150.42 cubic inches   = 35.2381 liters

Linear

1 inch (in.) = 2.540 centimeters (cm)
1 foot (ft.) = 0.3048 meter (m)
1 yard (yd.) = 0.9144 meter
1 rod (rd.) = 5.0292 meters
1 mile (mi.) = 1.6093 kilometers (km)

Liquid

1 fluidram (fl. dr.) =   0.2256 cubic inches (cu. in.) =   3.6967 milliliters (mL)
1 fluidounce (fl. oz.) =   1.8047 cubic inches   = 29.5727 milliliters
1 gill (gi.)   =   7.2188 cubic inches   = 118.2908 milliliters
1 pint (pt.)   = 28.8750 cubic inches   =   0.4732 liter (L)
1 quart (qt.)   = 57.7500 cubic inches   =   0.9463 liter
1 gallon (gal.)   = 231 cubic inches   =   3.7853 liters

Square or Surface

1 square inch (sq. in. or in²) = 6.4516 square centimeters (cm²)
1 square foot (sq. ft. or ft²) = 0.0929 square meters (m²)
1 square yard (sq. yd. or yd²) = 0.8361 square meters
1 square rod (sq. rd. or rd²)   = 25.2928 square meters
1 acre (A)   = 0.4047 hectare = 4,046.8564 square meters
1 square mile (sq. mi. or mi²) = 2.5900 square kilometers (km²)

Weight (Avoirdupois)

1 grain (gr.)   = 0.0648 gram (g)
1 dram (dr.)   = 1.7718 grams
1 ounce (oz.)   = 28.3495 grams
1 pound (lb.)   = 453.5924 grams
1 short ton (T.) = 0.9072 metric ton (t)
1 long ton (l.t.) = 1.01605 metric tons

Table II

Metric Units of Measure and Their Approximate U.S. Equivalents

Area

100 square millimeters (mm²)	= 1 sq. centimeter (cm²)	= 0.0001 m²	= 0.1550 sq. in.
100 square centimeters (cm²)	= 1 sq. decimeter (dm²)	= 0.01 m²	= 0.1076 sq. ft.
100 square decimeters (dm²)	= 1 centare* (ca)	= 1 m²	= 10.7639 sq. ft.
100 square meters (m²)	= 1 are* (a)	= 100 m²	= 119.5990 sq. yd.
100 ares (a)	= 1 hectare* (ha)	= 10 000 m²	= 2.4711 acres
100 hectares (ha)	= 1 sq. kilometer (km²)	= 1 000 000 m²	= 0.3861 sq. mi.

*Used in measuring land

Capacity

		Cubic	Dry	Liquid
	1 milliliter (mL)	= 0.0610 cu. in.		= 0.2705 fluidram
10 milliliters (mL)	= 1 centiliter (cL)	= 0.6102 cu. in.		= 0.3381 fl. oz.
10 centiliters (cL)	= 1 deciliter (dL)	= 6.1025 cu. in.	= 0.1816 pint	= 0.2113 pint
10 deciliters (dL)	= 1 liter (L)	= 61.0255 cu. in.	= 0.9081 quart	= 1.0567 quarts
10 liters (L)	= 1 dekaliter (daL)	= 0.3532 cu. ft.	= 1.1351 pecks	= 2.6418 gallons
10 dekaliters (daL)	= 1 hectoliter (hL)	= 3.5315 cu. ft.	= 2.8378 bushels	
10 hectoliters (hL)	= 1 kiloliter (kL)	= 1.3079 cu. yd.		

Linear

	1 millimeter (mm)	= 0.001 meter (m) =	0.0394 inch
10 millimeters (mm)	= 1 centimeter (cm)	= 0.01 meter =	0.3937 inch
10 centimeters (cm)	= 1 decimeter (dm)	= 0.1 meter =	3.9370 inches
10 decimeters (dm)	= 1 meter (m)	=	39.3701 inches
10 meters (m)	= 1 dekameter (dam)	= 10 meters =	32.8084 feet
10 dekameters (dam)	= 1 hectometer (hm)	= 100 meters =	328.0840 feet
10 hectometers (hm)	= 1 kilometer (km)	= 1 000 meters =	0.6214 mile

Weight (Mass)

	1 milligram (mg)	= 0.001 gram (g)	= 0.0154 grain
10 milligrams (mg)	= 1 centigram (cg)	= 0.01 gram	= 0.1543 grain
10 centigrams (cg)	= 1 decigram (dg)	= 0.1 gram	= 1.5432 grains
10 decigrams (dg)	= 1 gram (g)		= 0.0353 ounce
10 grams (g)	= 1 dekagram (dag)	= 10 grams	= 0.3527 ounce
10 dekagrams (dag)	= 1 hectogram (hg)	= 100 grams	= 3.5274 ounces
10 hectograms (hg)	= 1 kilogram (kg)	= 1 000 grams	= 2.2046 pounds
1 000 kilograms (kg)	= 1 metric ton (t)	= 1 000 000 grams	= 1.1023 tons